MOCK
THE
WEEK

First published 2009 by Boxtree
an imprint of Pan Macmillan Ltd
Pan Macmillan, 20 New Wharf Road, London N1 9RR
Basingstoke and Oxford
Associated companies throughout the world
www.panmacmillan.com

ISBN 978-0-7522-2695-8

9 8 7 6 5 4 3

A CIP catalogue record for this book is available from the British Library.

Design by Estuary English
Printed and bound by L.E.G.O. SpA, Italy

All photos courtesy of Shutterstock except: pp. 9/63 Alamy; pp. 84/137 iStock; p. 93 Alamy; pp. 12/15/24/27/44/69/70/78/105/112/115/125/141/145 Estuary English

THIS YEAR'S BOOK

ALL-NEW SCENES WE'D LIKE TO SEE

EWAN PHILLIPS, DAN PATTERSON, SIMON BULLIVANT, ROB COLLEY, DAN GASTER, GED PARSONS, GILES PILBROW, STEVE PUNT AND COLIN SWASH

BOXTREE

CONTENTS

1. UNLIKELY DICTIONARY DEFINITIONS

bestiality (*noun*): an act of sexual congress with an animal, disgusting, you need help. Pervert. I don't know why I married you, I'm calling the police.

birdflu (*noun*): fictitious disease that will supposedly wipe out the Earth at any time soon, *see also*: SARS, swine flu, ebola, flesh-eating virus, MRSA, global warming, nuclear war, grey goo, dirty bombs, supergun, ricin, dangerous dogs, Boris Johnson, etc.

catchasnatch (*noun*): 1. medieval dagger. 2. nickname for Roman emperor. 3. term used in graphic design … Frank Muir?

celebrity (*noun*): anyone.

dictionary (*noun*): book with words in. I imagine you already knew that or you wouldn't have bought this. Lifelong work for the likes of me, I'm not complaining, like, but obviously when I started out I wanted to be a novelist.

fart (*noun*): expulsion of trapped methane from the anus, possibly the funniest thing ever.

fisting (*verb*): what are you doing even looking this up?

fromage (*noun*): something which is smellier, uglier and more expensive in France, like their women.

leather (*noun*): material for garments, as in trousers and underwear, feels good, ooh, mmm.

miscagnate (*verb*): I've just no idea what this means, sorry.

misogynist (*noun*): someone who, for perfectly valid reasons, usually bitter experience, especially expensive divorce, hates women, they're all whores.

nadir (*noun*): the opposite of zenith, the lowest or most unsuccessful point, the ITV sitcom *Teenage Kicks*.

nipple clamp (*noun*): mine's killing me.

paedophile (*noun*): misunderstood, needlessly victimized, she told me she was sixteen.

poo (*noun*): 1. something you shit out, you can get big ones, runny ones or little pellet things (can be hard to flush). 2. Term of abuse, as in: 'That Hitler was a real poo.' 3. Sometimes with the suffix –f, meaning a gay man. (*Shak.*) A poo, a poo, my kingdom for a poo (*Richard III*, Act V Scene 4). I think it's time I retired from this job … (*Donne*) No poo is an island, entire of itself. (*Nurs. rhyme*) Humpty Dumpty sat on a poo. (*Comic book*) Batman & Poo. Endlessly amusing especially if you're a boy or if you spend all day writing a boring fucking dictionary. P.S. You're fired. (*Editor*.)

Ray Stubbs (*noun*): sexy beast, e.g. 'You turn me on like Ray Stubbs.'

verb (*noun*): a word that describes, you know, things, like, you know, verbs and stuff.

willy (*noun*): pfft, tee hee.

2. UNLIKELY THINGS TO READ ON A MOTORWAY SIGN (Part 1)

SO I CAN TYPE ANYTHING IN HERE AND IT COMES UP ON A SIGN ON THE M6? REALLY?

MIKE ROBINSON WANTS TO BE YOUR FRIEND. CONFIRM?

TIME TO JUNCTION FIFTEEN: 28 MINUTES. SEE IF YOU CAN DO IT IN 20.

FUCK ALL OF YOU.

MEN SITTING IN STATIONARY JCBS SMOKING AND READING THE *SUN* FOR NEXT 29 MILES.

YOU THOUGHT YOU'D GOT RID OF ME WHEN WE WERE DIVORCED BUT I'M STILL WATCHING YOU.

DON'T DRIVE TIRED. PULL IN FOR A RED BULL AND VODKA AT JUNCTION 8.

HONK IF YOU'VE HAD IT TODAY.

MAJOR ROADWORKS AHEAD. EXPECT DELAYS UNTIL 2065.

NO OVERTAKING. NO BLACKS. NO IRISH. NO DOGS.

BEWARE: PEOPLE DRIVING LIKE C**TS AHEAD.

LIVERPOOL 6, MANCHESTER 8. HA! TAKE THAT, RAFA!

DANGER: FOG. SHROUDING THE ROAD AHEAD LIKE GREAT WHITE FURS, SLIPPING STEALTHILY DOWN FROM THE CROW-BLACK EMBANKMENTS ON TO THE ENDLESSLY UNRAVELLING DAMASK OF THE MOTORWAY.

YUK - LOOK AT THAT
I THINK IT'S A FOX
100 YARDS

3. REJECTED EXAM QUESTIONS (Part 1)

1. Put these queens of England in the order you would shag them.
2. Paul has a cake. He gives Peter $^4/_9$ of it, he gives Mary $^1/_{12}$ of it, he then gives Barry $^2/_7$ of it and Frances the rest. Can you diagnose which mental illness he is clearly suffering from?
3. In nothing did Louis XIV err more than his policy on the Church. Illustrate using potato prints and glitter.
4. Will this exam paper be marked before the end of the summer holidays? Discuss.
5. *Mansfield Park* is set neither in Mansfield nor a park. What the fuck is Jane Austen on about?
6. Using the weapon provided, run amok in the exam room making reference to the government, Jesus and your over-protective parents.
7. Black music is better than white music. Diss.
8. When in Rome, you see a man shit in the street. What should you do?
9. Complete the following line of poetry: 'There was a young man from Bangkok …'
10. Discuss Shakespeare's use of the word 'c**t' in *Romeo and Juliet.*
11. Terry has translated Hamlet's soliloquy, changing all the letter Bs to Cs, and Anne has translated Coleridge's *Kubla Khan*, replacing all As with Ts. How much of their lives has been a waste?

12. Cakes are nice, aren't they?

13. Frank Lampard is taking a corner in front of you. Give five off-colour examples of things you should direct at him. Extra points given for objects, bodily fluids and filthy songs.

14. Draw a diagram of the female reproductive organs, using the sheets provided to wipe up your jizz afterwards.

15. My dog has got no nose. Please show how it smells using a diagram.

16. John travels 5 miles to work, where he earns £10. Can't he do better than that?

17. How many sexual partners have you had? Please give details in your answer.

18. 'Henry VIII's wives got what they deserved by and large.' Discuss without using the word 'slags'.

19. Everything in history is Britain's fault. Agree.

20. If John earns £300 and buys a DVD for £100, how much was he ripped off?

21. If George takes 65 tablets and Sally swallows 25 tablets, how good is your alibi going to have to be?

22. If John has five potatoes and Colin has four, how long before Channel 4 makes a documentary about them called *Jamie's Potato-Addicted Teens*?

4. CARDS YOU NEVER SEE IN A NEWSAGENT'S WINDOW (Part 1)

FRENCH TUTOR:
GIVEZ-MOI UNE
CALL MAINTENANT

ADMINISTRATIVE / FINANCE ASSISTANT

REQUIRED

RS PER WEEK

LY MON – FRI

am to 2pm

WANT COCK? MEET ME OUTSIDE HERE AT 2 A.M. ON TUESDAY.

CAR BOOT. WOULD SUIT PERSON WITH REST OF CAR.

WHAT ARE YOU LOOKING AT?

BUILDER AVAILABLE, AS SEEN ON TV (IN ITV'S *COWBOYS, CROOKS AND CONMEN*).

ASK YOUR NEWSAGENT TO EXPLAIN THE COMPLEXITIES OF THE CURRENT GAZA CONFLICT.

CHILD MINDER AVAILABLE – HE MAY BE SMALL BUT HE'S ROCK HARD.

LIKE ANTIQUES? SOME OF OUR CRISPS ARE OVER TWO YEARS OLD.

SCHOOL CHILDREN: JUST TWO AT A TIME PLEASE. THERE'S ONLY SO MUCH OF ME TO GO ROUND.

COME IN AND 'BROWSE'.

BIRTHDAY CARD FOR SALE, WOULD SUIT SOMEONE CALLED KEN.

MATHS TUTOR AVAILABLE 25/7.

BONA FIDE JULIUS CAESAR'S ORIGINAL LATIN DICTIONARY FOR SALE. CAVEAT EMPTOR.

KNITTER? PERVERT? COME TO THE STITCH 'N' FIST AT THE VILLAGE HALL, THURSDAY NIGHTS 8 P.M.

5. THINGS YOU WON'T HEAR IN A RADIO TRAFFIC REPORT

'Unless you clear the M25, Chris Moyles gets it.'

'And there is now a 20-mile tailback caused by the wreckage of my helicopter.'

'Beep! Same to you, you fat twat, learn how to drive ...'

'There is currently a queue of four cars at the traffic lights on the High Street.'

'There's pandemonium below me, fire, smoke, loud bangs ... we appear to be flying over Basra. Steve, what are you bloody doing?'

'If you're heading south clockwise on the M25, what the fuck are you doing, you maniac? You're going to cause a crash!'

'... and a message to Dave back in the studio: Dave, if you put on James Blunt one more time, we're going to strafe your mum's house.'

'And from this helicopter, I can clearly see my urine splashing on the roofs of the cars queuing on the M5.'

'Some old bastard is attempting to reverse park his Volvo outside Pizza Express, he's never going to get it in there, stay with me and we'll see if he does.'

'Launch missile. Fire 1!'

'Don't go on the M25 between Junctions 7 and 11 tonight, it is absolutely bumper-to-bumper, all four lanes closed. OK, we off air, Jim? Great, that should leave my journey home clear again.'

'And hilariously, on the van in front someone has written: "I wish my wife was as dirty as this," and he's written it in the dirt on the back door. Brilliant.'

'Traffic report and I'm in a fucking helicopter, no one told me about this, I hate heights.'

'So, carnage on the M1, at least ten people dead. Here's Katie Melua.'

'If you're on the North Circular heading towards Palmers Green, watch out by the Asda, there's a woman waiting to cross with amazing tits.'

'Mrs Jones is currently waiting for the bin lorry to move from the middle of Fir Tree Avenue.'

'As we put on "Ride of the Valkyries", we're going to swoop down and take out some gooks with a chopper.'

'They look like ants down there, oh, apparently they are ants, we haven't taken off yet.'

'Sometimes when I am up here circling, gazing down at the cars trundling along the highways, I have this overwhelming urge just to ram this fucker into a building.'

'We have problems on the M1, M3, M4, M6 and M11 – and that concludes tomorrow's traffic report.'

'Traffic slow below me – mainly as they're watching me bungee jumping out of this helicopter.'

'It's only taken me two minutes to get to Tower Bridge this morning, but then I am in a helicopter.'

6. THINGS TO SAY THAT WILL CHANGE THE ATMOSPHERE AT A DINNER PARTY (Part 1)

'I think I'm comfortably the richest person here.'

'That's it with just a semi on ...'

'I know you're a granny now, but when you were young, did you like bum love?'

'Now, does everyone eat pig snout?'

'You know the bin Ladens, don't you, Mr Bush? Just don't mention 9/11, they're very touchy.'

'I've underestimated a little bit, so I'll have to give you a smaller portion, Mr Prescott.'

'Yes, I have got smallpox, but don't worry, if you've already had it you won't catch it.'

'Amy, they're here to take you back to rehab.'

'This is Pete Best, everyone. No jokes about the Beatles!'

'Anyone up for Islamic Pictionary?'

'Who had the chicken? An ambulance is on the way.'

'Yes, I am *that* John Leslie.'

'Mmm, this satay nut roast is delicious – there aren't any nuts in it, are there?'

'My secret ingredient? I poach the fish in its own semen.'

'Before the cheese course we always pass round the smack.'

'No, I'll use the downstairs toilet, and leave the door open – that way we can carry on the conversation.'

'Are the Mafia still after you?'

'I am Mephisto and whoever ate the minestrone made a tacit bargain with me.'

'Have you met Lord and Lady Lucan?'

'Oh, that. That's just the volcano the house is built on.'

'There's a space over next to Heather, Sir Paul.'

'Can anyone else do this with their dick?'

7. UNLIKELY OBITUARIES (Part 1)

IN MEMORIAM

The world will be a sadder place without him, though not significantly.

Good riddance to the old c**t.

He had a chequered career. Or, in other words, he was a crook.

This 'talentless, callow, backstabbing bastard', as he would like to be remembered.

She was a major screen star of the forties and was thought to be one of Britain's greatest beauties, but time wasn't kind to her, and by the time I shagged her, she was absolutely hideous.

Died suddenly and peacefully on an electric chair at the New York State Penitentiary.

The less said about him, the better.

The inventor of Cluedo, died in the conservatory, with a cardiac arrest.

He leaves a wife, two children and a bullet hole, along with a series of blood stains on his bedroom wall.

Some said he was unwise to criticize President Putin ...

He leaves a wife, two children and absolutely fuck all to me, his supposed best friend.

He was a brash, flamboyant personality who didn't suffer fools gladly – a shit, in other words.

He has left a fortune of £100 million under his bed – finders keepers!

Born in 1873, he would have been 135, so that must be a mistake.

8. UNNERVING THINGS TO HEAR IN A MEDICAL EXAM (Part 1)

'Nurse, can you get the senior consultant, and tell him to run like fuck.'

'Can you cover one eye and read this in a sexy French accent?'

'I've run out of lubricant, so I'm going to spit on my finger.'

'I've never seen a shadow that big. Ah, panic over, there's a spider on the lens.'

'Nurse – the screens! The football's about to start.'

'I'm now going to num your vagina ... num num num.'

'I think there is a clinic that can deal with an emergency like this, but it's in rural Japan.'

'Can you climb up this ladder and shit into this bucket?'

'Well, I'm surprised, but I'm afraid you've got testicular cancer, Mrs Smith.'

'Just out of interest, do you have any favourite hymns or poems?'

'So, if you could just pop my clothes off ...'

'Your bones appear to be made from a substance not known on this planet.'

'Yes, Siree, I taught myself all the fancy doctorin' I needs to know.'

'So, how bad is this premature ... eeeeargh!'

'Aha, malignant. Yes! That's ten quid the radiologist owes me.'

'Stand back, nurse, I'm going to pop it.'

'Right, Mrs Jones, if you could just take your bra off we'll have a look at that ingrowing toenail of yours.'

'Now we're going to test your sphincter control.'

'Close your eyes, open your mouth and start sucking when I give the signal.'

9. UNLIKELY THINGS TO HEAR IN A PORN FILM

'Can't we get on with it? I'm red raw.'

'There you go, Fräulein, I have fixed your dishwasher. Goodbye!'

'Is this based on a true story?'

'Fuck! I think I've snapped my banjo string.'

'Is it in yet?'

'Is Pandora Peaks your real name?'

'I'm really annoyed that Tim Burton stole the plot of Edward Penishands *and made his own version.'*

'Sorry, love, it slipped up there by accident.'

'Sex? Is it my birthday?'

'Well, strictly missionary, turn the lights off and you can only do it through a hole in a sheet.'

'My contract says no nudity.'

'This has never happened to me before.'

'Your breasts look so real.'

'This blow job scene just doesn't seem to be essential to the plot.'

10. TEXT MESSAGES THEY JUST MISSED

Mr al Fayed, we've just crashed in Paris, it was all an accident and by the way, I'm not pregnant or engaged, love Diana

Gordon, I'd call an election now if I were you, think the economy is going to go tits up. Love Tony

Romeo, am in the crypt but am not dead, just wait 4 me 2 wake up, love Juliet xx

I'm still in that same cave just by the Khyber Pass – will be there until next Tuesday. Osama

This is the FIrsst evur t extmessage sent

Jon, you've left a CD-ROM with loads of personal details of benefit claimants in the pub

Oedipus. She's your real mum mate. Oops bit late now. Lol. Polybus

Britney, you've forgotten your knickers, careful getting out of your car

Dear Mr Litvinenko, tea and sushi meeting is off this morning

I'm texting you from the car behind, my brakes have failed and I can't slow down, get out of the wa ...

Mr President, you should probably pop down to New Orleans and help out after the hurricane. Your advisors

Jesus, avoid the Garden of Gethsemane tonight, will explain later. Judas

11. UNLIKELY THINGS TO FIND WRITTEN ON A SHAMPOO BOTTLE

TESTED ON ANIMALS. THEIR EYES FELL OUT
BUT THEIR HAIR LOOKED LOVELY.

CONTAINS EXTRACT OF AVOCADO – THOUGH TO BE HONEST WE'VE
NO IDEA IF THAT'S A GOOD THING OR NOT.

MAY CONTAIN TRACES OF ASBESTOS.

FOR REALLY DISGUSTING, GREASY HAIR.

40% PROOF.

SEE DOCTOR IN CASE OF CONTACT WITH SKIN.

CAUTION: DO NOT GET WET.

WHY ARE YOU READING THIS SHAMPOO BOTTLE?

YOUR HAIR IS SHIT.

INSTRUCTIONS FOR USE: IT'S SHAMPOO, FOR CHRIST'S SAKE!
WORK IT OUT FOR YOURSELF.

IDEAL FOR ITCHY SCALPS. GUARANTEED TO GIVE YOU ONE.

CONTAINS ESSENTIAL OILS FOR SHINY HAIR AND A WET NOSE.

WITH EXTRACT OF VANILLA, FOR PEOPLE WHO LIKE THEIR HAIR TO
SMELL LIKE CUSTARD.

CONTENTS: SHAMPOO.

FOR MATURE LADIES, TO HELP COLOUR THOSE GREY HAIRS.
ALSO AVAILABLE IN MINGE-SIZED BOTTLES.

CONTAINS EXTRACT OF JOJOBA, AND EXTRACT OF HOBO.

MAY CAUSE ALOPECIA.

12. UNLIKELY PROPERTY MAGAZINE ADVERTS (Part 1)

• FOR SALE

House for sale, £25 ONO, original swing bin and will throw in Bounty kitchen towel.

Opportunity to purchase unique detached corrugated iron residence in London's hip up-and-coming Little Darfur region.

Enviable beachfront property benefiting from recent sudden change in location from top to bottom of cliff. In need of some rebuilding.

First time on the market since last week when I bought it off a senile old woman and am now flogging it for £100,000 more.

A once in a lifetime opportunity to purchase a secluded woodland mansion unexpectedly available due to horrendous bloodbath of previous owner and family. Twenty-five-year lease, or 16 if he behaves himself in prison.

Get in first – unbelievable apartment, very quiet, particularly after Lights Out or during Sedation Hour. Planning permission pending for conversion from asylum.

Imposing, beautiful ambassador-style residence – 6 bedrooms, 4 reception rooms, 6,000 square feet, beautiful garden, planning permission for toilet (in Hampstead's famous no-lavatory conservation area).

Move up in the world. This beautiful residence boasts 15 bedrooms, indoor pool, leisure complex and parking for 20 cars – OK, it's a room at the Holiday Inn Birmingham.

FOR SALE: designer family home on private island, swimming pool/rocket launchpad. Apply J. Tracey.

Bijou apartment in highly desirable area of North London, so neighbours likely to be c**ts.

Spacious white-painted, timber-framed home, on top of large pole. Charming rustic design. 1 foot by 2. Would suit dove.

Four houses for sale – Whitechapel Road – upgrading to hotel. Dogs and top hats must not apply.

TO LET: deceptively spacious accommodation, blue wooden exterior. Ideal for policeman, or Time Lord.

Large, well-appointed dog, would suit family of fleas. Short walk to park, no chain.

FOR SALE: house. Slightly bleak. Apply C. Dickens.

Large timber-framed houseboat. Very roomy, 40 cubits by 20. Pets welcome. Leasehold 40 days and 40 nights. Apply Noah.

Small but desirable home, convenient for City and West End, located just south of Zimbabwe's main airport.

13. LINES CUT FROM A SUPERHERO FILM

'YOU KNOW BATMAN, SOMETIMES YOU REMIND ME OF THAT PONCEY RICH TWAT BRUCE WAYNE.'

'SORRY, LOIS, I DID WARN YOU I WAS FASTER THAN A SPEEDING BULLET.'

'UNFORTUNATELY, SUPERMAN WAS USING HIS X-RAY VISION AND HAS FLOWN DIRECTLY INTO THAT WALL.'

'HOLY INAPPROPRIATE, BATMAN, YOU'RE HURTING ME!'

'SORRY, I'VE GOT WEB ALL OVER THE SHEETS, I'LL SLEEP IN THAT BIT.'

'LOOK, COMMISSIONER GORDON, I DON'T WANT TO GIVE YOU ADVICE, BUT COULD WE NOT KEEP THE JOKER, THE RIDDLER AND THE PENGUIN IN PRISON FOR MORE THAN A WEEK?'

'HOW UNLUCKY – HE ESCAPED TO EARTH FROM HIS DOOMED PLANET BUT HIS CAPSULE LANDED ON KRAKATOA AT THE PRECISE MOMENT IT ERUPTED.'

'I PUT OUT THE FIRE LOIS, BY EJACULATING OVER IT FROM MY SUPER GONADS.'

'CATWOMAN, WILL YOU USE THE LITTER TRAY, FOR FUCK'S SAKE.'

'IT'S A SHAME THAT THERE'S ONE BIT OF YOUR BODY THAT DOESN'T EXTEND, ELASTIC MAN.'

'THIS SOUNDS LIKE A JOB FOR SEQUEL MAN 3, WHO'S GOOD,

BUT NOT QUITE AS GOOD AS SEQUEL MAN 2.'

'I HAVE FURTHER EVIDENCE THAT BATMAN HIT MY CLIENT, M'LUD. EXHIBIT THREE: A LARGE SIGN SAYING, "WHACK".'

'I'VE USED MY LASER VISION TO MICROWAVE THAT SANDWICH.'

'YOU'RE NOT EXACTLY STRIKING FEAR INTO THE HEARTS OF THE CITY'S CRIMINALS, MEDIOCREMAN.'

'HOW EXACTLY DO YOU FLY, CAPTAIN FLATULENCE?'

'LOOK! THERE! IN THE SKY! IS IT A BIRD? IS IT A PLANE? NO, IT'S BIRDPLANE MAN!'

'DR BANNER, I'M AFRAID YOU CAN'T COME TO MY ANGER MANAGEMENT SEMINAR ANY MORE.'

'WE'RE THE X MEN AND WE'RE LOOKING FOR OUR X WIVES.'

'HOLY FUCKING SHIT, BATMAN.'

'I USED TO BE FASTER THAN A SPEEDING BULLET, BUT I DID MY ANTERIOR CRUCIATE LIGAMENT.'

'ACCORDING TO MY X-RAY VISION, YOU REQUIRE A FILLING IN YOUR RIGHT UPPER MOLAR.'

'A HAPPY FINISH, PLEASE, ALFRED.'

'HOLLYWOOD SEEMS TO BE DOWN TO THE LESS WELL-KNOWN MARVEL CHARACTERS NOW, SCRAPING THE BARREL MAN ...'

'WE'VE HAD TO LET THE JOKER GO UNDER THE HUMAN RIGHTS ACT.'

'YOU'RE LATE, VIRGINTRAINMAN.'

'ROBIN, STOP BEING A BAT C**T.'

14. THINGS THAT WOULD RUIN A MEAL IN A RESTAURANT (Part 1)

'Let me order for you, darling ... The lady will have the cheapest thing on the menu, please.'

'This year we put our own excrement on the organic vegetable patch.'

'Is it me or does that sauce look like a burst abscess?'

'The next table said it's Mafia justice, but it'll be over soon.'

'I can see you were annoyed and I will replace your meal. Now, would you rather Chef spat, pissed or wanked in your soup?'

'That Casserole Cannibale was delicious, what was in it?'

'Would you like to choose a turkey for us to strangle for you?'

'Excuse me, waiter, it's my wedding anniversary today, so can you hurry up with the lady's dessert, I've got to get home to the wife ...'

'We've roped that area off for the Hideous Skin Complaint Party.'

'Would Sir like to pull the sausage out of my arse now?'

'Here's the wine list, Sir, it's quite short: red, white or Blue Nun?'

'Are you the one who got me a written warning last week? Enjoy your steak.'

'I've got some spinach in my teeth – you don't mind if I take them out and clean them, do you?'

'No, I haven't farted; I have, in fact, shat myself.'

'Keep an eye out for Chef's blue elastoplast.'

'Mr Ramsay's coming to deal with your complaint personally.'

'Would you like to see our bulimic menu, Madam?'

'Help yourself at the salad bar – it's over there by the gents.'

'I couldn't help noticing Madam's backside as she walked in – are you sure you won't have the salad?'

'So, this peanut allergy of yours – how bad is it?'

'Each one of those apricots has been sucked by the chef and checked for flavour.'

15. UNLIKELY AGONY AUNT LETTERS

★★★ *Star Letter* ★★★

Dear Agony Aunt,
I keep getting dangerous advice from hugely unqualified people – what do you suggest I do?

Dear Agony Aunt,
Please help me, I can't stop making up bullshit problems and sending them to newspaper agony aunts.

Dear Agony Aunt,
I think my wife may no longer love me. I enclose a series of pictures of her in her underwear and me in briefs discussing our problems, which you might want to turn into a photo story.

Dear Agony Aunt,
I can't stop masturbating over agony aunt columns.

Dear Agony Aunt,
I have a very tiny penis, which is not good – but I am a woman, which is worse.

Dear Agony Aunt,
I am worried about losing some sensitive government data that it is my job to safeguard, so I have sent it to you to look after.

Dear Agony Aunt,
Is it true you can't get pregnant if your boyfriend gives you an STD?

Dear Agony Aunt,
this is a genuine letter.

Dear Agony Aunt,
I'm having an affair with the husband of your paper's agony aunt.

Dear Agony Aunt,
I have a problem with premature ejaculation ... whoops, sorry, have to go now.

Dead Aguny Arnt,
My spell chocker brock, whit shull I do?

Dear Agony Aunt,
I'm a serial killer obsessed with stalking and then killing agony aunts. I am typing this on your home computer.

Dear Agony Aunt,
It's tough being the world's most intelligent dog.

Auntie,
I'm in agony, love,
Your Nephew.

Dear Agony Aunt,
I am painfully shy – will it do me any good to publicize my problem in a national newspaper?

Dear Agony Aunt,
I am not quite pretty enough to appear on page three – can you please use me in one of your photo stories?

Dear Agony Aunt,
I'm a gay man, but I'm neither witty nor stylish – am I secretly straight?

★★★ *£10 Prize* ★★★

Dear Agony Aunt,
I suffer from Tourette's, you fucking ct.**

16. UNLIKELY THINGS TO READ IN A FORTUNE COOKIE

You're Fucked

We are from the planet Snack, that cookie was our leader

You've eaten this without opening it, you greedy bastard

You have just paid over the odds for a mediocre Chinese meal

Prepare to die

Help, I'm trapped in a fortune-cookie factory

If you've come here for a meal on Valentine's night, I imagine you must be trapped in a loveless marriage and yearning to stray

You are about to give the waiter a huge tip

You thought that pork looked like dog

Yes, we have nice food, but a questionable record on human rights

An anvil is suspended above your head. Don't look up – any sudden movement could release it

In order to read this, you have obliterated the cookie, you heartless bastard

Your cookie will now self-destruct

You have been charged £10 for this cookie

You are gay

You are about to read this out in a pathetic attempt at a Chinese accent and may prefix it with: 'Confucius he say ...'

This cookie is radioactive

Goodbye cruel world, Love, Your Cookie

17. UNLIKELY LINES FROM A SCI-FI FILM
(Part 1)

'QUICK, HIS BATTERY IS RUNNING OUT!'

'ON MY PLANET, THIS IS CONSIDERED A BIG DICK.'

'I THINK I'VE DISCOVERED THE MONSTER'S WEAKNESS – IT'S THE ZIP AT THE BACK.'

'THIS IS THE PLANET ONAN, THE LOCALS DIED OUT... UNSURPRISINGLY.'

'LOOK, WE CAN TRANSPORT MATTER ACROSS THE GALAXY WITH THIS NEW "FAX" MACHINE.'

'YOUR ALIEN LANGUAGE DOESN'T USE THE LETTERS K OR Z.'

'MR SPOCK, YOU HAVE THE BRIDGE. I'M JUST GOING FOR A DUMP.'

'LOOK, FOR THE LAST TIME, A LIGHT YEAR IS A UNIT OF DISTANCE, NOT TIME.'

'I AM FROM THE PLANET MINGE.'

'I FEEL A GREAT DISTURBANCE IN THE FORCE, LUKE – IT'S ALMOST AS IF SOMEONE'S PLANNING ON MAKING THREE DREADFUL PREQUELS.'

'LUKE, I AM YOUR FATHER, COUSIN, UNCLE AND BROTHER.'

'I DON'T WISH TO CRITICIZE, LORD VADER – BUT I DON'T THINK A CAPE IS TERRIBLY PRACTICAL FOR SPACE TRAVEL.'

'WE'RE FLYING BACK ON EASYUFO, SO WE AREN'T LANDING ON MARS, WE'RE ACTUALLY LANDING ON SATURN AND GOING THE REST OF THE WAY BY COACH.'

'I AM FROM THE FUTURE AND I'VE BEEN SENT BACK AS A MATTER OF URGENCY TO KILL GILLIAN McKEITH.'

'THIS IS DARTH, EVERYONE. IF YOU'D LIKE TO SIT NEXT TO THE SKYWALKERS, I'LL PUT JABBA IN BETWEEN THE WAN KENOBIS.'

'ON MY PLANET, EARTH, YOUNG WOMEN GREET MEN BY PUTTING THIS IN THEIR MOUTHS AND SUCKING REPEATEDLY...'

'I TOLD YOU WE SHOULD HAVE GOT PETROL ON JUPITER, BUT OH NO, MR KNOWITALL HAD TO CUT IT FINE...'

'WE ARE FROM THE PLANET GAY, WE ARE DYING OUT BUT HAVE BEAUTIFUL FURNISHINGS AND A SHOWTUNE COLLECTION THAT IS SECOND TO NONE.'

18. LINES YOU WOULDN'T WANT TO HEAR IN A COSTUME DRAMA (Part 1)

'Why, Mr Darcy, I declare from your breeches you have a cock the size of a baby's arm holding a peach.'

'Candleford's a bit of a shithole, isn't it? I'm moving to Lark Rise.'

'Well, it may be Bleak, but it's not got planning permission.'

'Yes, I shall marry you! I shall be proud to carry the name of Mrs Pockle-Thickle-Facklethwaite.'

'Miss Dashwood, I've brought round a Chinese.'

'Robin Steven Hood, I am arresting you on a charge of robbing the rich to give to the poor. You have the right to remain silent.'

'Forget about who dances with whom at some stupid sodding ball, woman, we're at war with France!'

'Why, Miss Steadman, I've forgotten which Dickens book we're in this week.'

'The main Lark Rise to Candleford road is closed this morning after a stagecoach jack-knifed and shed its load of bonnet-wearing spinsters.'

'Sorry, Mr Rochester, I'm not putting out until your wife snuffs it.'

'Why, Mr Darcy, you're piss-wet through.'

'Pls sir. I wd luv some more. Txt me back lol.'

'OK, Oliver, can you show us where Mr Bumble touched you?'

'The Casterbridge Mayoral race has been thrown wide open now Boris has joined and the current Mayor is being done for funding issues.'

'We've come to take the telly and the sofa, Mrs Bennett.'

'Is it true what they say about you Cranford girls?'

'Oh, Mr Micawber, when you said something would come up I didn't realize you meant that!'

'Yo, Mr Rochester, you is one slim'assed motherfucker.'

'Oh, Heathcliffe, do me up the wrong'un!'

19. UNLIKELY QUIZ SHOW QUESTIONS

'Let's have a look at what you could have won if you'd been on a better show.'

'The phone lines are open now with the question: how long will you be prepared to hold at £1.80 a minute?'

'The answers to those last questions were: cancer, and the Holocaust. Join us after the break when we'll be playing Pin the Jelly to the Wall!'

'What am I? No, it was a good guess, but "a very lucky, talentless wannabe who has blow-jobbed his way to the top" is not the right answer.'

'Is this a question?'

'You're watching Challenge TV, and you're playing for a jackpot of £1.50.'

'Are you gay? That's a question from your mum and dad, also signed by your wife.'

'"Something you would keep secret from your wife." You said, "I shagged her sister at her fortieth birthday party." Our survey said, "You silly bastard, you weren't meant to be quite so specific."'

'With reference to the criticism and the play itself, consider the ways in which our fascination with *Hamlet* depends on our tendency to identify with the character of Hamlet.'

'OK, and whoever is left unable to answer when the clock is ticking must eat the soggy biscuit. You know the rules.'

'How big is my cock?'

'Dan, you are the weakest link. You were … shit. Sorry, I've just run out of insults.'

'OK, your starter for ten: who is better, me or Bamber Gascoigne?'

'For ten points: is my career in the toilet?'

'Welcome to *The Weakest Link*. Your first question: do you fantasize about me in leather holding a whip?'

'Name something you'd find.'

'We asked you to complete the phrase: "Hand –" for £50,000. None of you got the answer, which was "Hand Amputation".'

'If I said you had a beautiful body, would you hold it against me?'

'How small is too small?'

'Let's play *The Weakest Link*. What "B" do I regularly inject into my forehead?'

'Complete the name of the famous double act: Ant and a) Dec, b) Dave.'

'You have two minutes on your specialist subject: the sex life of John Humphries.'

'For a million pounds, what's the best way to cheat on *Millionaire*? Is it a) cough ...'

'Okay, for a million pounds ... I'm hosting this quiz show.'

'So, you have a choice of molecular physics, ancient Greek poetry or *Big Brother* winners.'

'Welcome to the specialist knowledge round. Your first question on your chosen subject: what is the fastest way to dispose of a dead body without the use of acid?'

'Well, Dafydd Griffiths, you've won a week's holiday in ... Wales! How do you feel?'

'Sorry, but that top prize I said was yours to keep whatever happens? You've just lost it.'

'You scored eighteen points on *Holby City* 2004–2005, and nothing on general knowledge.'

'OK, King's College, Cambridge: how was *Chris Moyles's Quiz Night* ever commissioned?'

20. UNLIKELY THINGS TO HEAR IN A WAR FILM (Part 1)

'CAN YOU HEAR THE DRUMS, FERNANDO?'

'YESTERDAY I KILLED A MAN FOR THE FIRST TIME – IT GAVE ME A HARD ON.'

'WELL, IT STARTED OUT AS A TUNNEL, BUT SINCE IT COLLAPSED IT'S SORT OF BECOME A GRAVE FOR GINGER.'

'BAD NEWS, LADS, THE ESCAPE TUNNEL'S COME OUT IN ANOTHER PRISONER-OF-WAR CAMP.'

'ALL RIGHT, MEN, THE NIGHT BEFORE THE BIG PUSH, WHY DON'T WE ALL HAVE A CUDDLE?'

'THAT'S UNLUCKY, PARACHUTING OUT SAFELY AND LANDING ON A PITCHFORK.'

'THE GOOD NEWS IS WE'VE BLOWN THE DAM UP. THE BAD NEWS IS THAT IT WAS THE SEVERN, NOT THE RHINE.'

'OK, MEN, FIRST DAY OF THE SOMME CAMPAIGN. YOU GO AHEAD WITHOUT ME, I'VE GOT A BIT OF A JIPPY TUMMY.'

'YOU KNOW – IN TEN YEARS' TIME OUR ECONOMY WILL HAVE COLLAPSED AND GERMANY'S WILL BE THE STRONGEST IN EUROPE.'

'I DO WANT TO FIND PRIVATE RYAN, SIR, BUT I JUST CAN'T TAKE YOU SERIOUSLY AFTER *FORREST GUMP*.'

'I'LL NEED SOME VOLUNTEERS FOR THIS SUICIDE MISSION. WELL DONE, AHMED.'

'BLOWING UP THIS DAM IS A VITAL MISSION – IT WILL DRAIN THE ENTIRE RESERVOIR AND DENY THE GERMANS MUCH-NEEDED CANOEING AND WATER-SKIING FACILITIES.'

'DON'T WORRY, THE BELGIAN DEFENCES WILL HOLD THEM UP – BLIMEY, THAT WAS QUICK.'

'AH, YOU MUST BE THE FAMOUS DOUGLAS BADER. DON'T GET UP.'

'OK, MEN. WE'RE ABOUT TO GO OVER THE TOP. WE CAN'T HELP IT WITH DANIEL DAY LEWIS IN THE CAST.'

'I LOVE THE SMELL OF NAPALM IN THE MORNINGS – FAILING THAT, A FRESHLY BAKED ALMOND CROISSANT AND A LATTE.'

'BAD NEWS, CHAPS – THE GREAT ESCAPE HAS FAILED. HOW ABOUT WE TRY IT AGAIN NEXT BANK HOLIDAY?'

'LOOK, THERE'S ONLY ONE WAY WE'RE EVER GOING TO WIN THIS MATCH AGAINST THE GERMANS – STALLONE, YOU GO UP FRONT – AND PELE, GET IN GOAL.'

'ER, HANNIBAL – YOU KNOW THOSE BUNS WE WERE SAVING FOR WHEN WE GOT OVER THE ALPS...?'

21. UNLIKELY THINGS TO FIND WRITTEN ON TOILET PAPER PACKAGING (Part 1)

Degradable packaging

INSTRUCTIONS
Wipe bottom, drop into toilet, flush, repeat

New Extra Strong for those frenzied teenage wanks

New sandpaper softness

New 4-ply for those tiny little ones that smear out of all control

Buy two Shitaways, get one Snotaway free!

Low fat

However beautiful she might be, she'll still use this. Get 'Lady Lav' for the woman in your life

New Parental Control toilet paper, with semen-activated alarm system

Andrex Brown – for the really stubborn stains

Just add gravy

New Gillian McKeith loo roll, assesses your diet as you wipe

New Sat Lav – woman's voice directs you to bits you may have missed

Flypaper Loo, an end to sticky clagnuts for ever

Man Rag – for the arsehole in your life

New Two-Way Wax n' Wipe, cleans your bottom and shaves your sack and crack

With new fragrance: shit

22. THINGS YOU DON'T WANT TO HEAR IN A PSYCHIATRIST'S OFFICE

'Look at this inkblot of two lesbians doing it and tell me what you see.'

'Hello? Hello?! What sort of a greeting is that? You're obviously a closet homosexual with an Oedipus complex.'

'You think you've got troubles ...'

'I insist on all my female patients taking their tops off. Flub-lb-lb-lb.'

'I'll need to strap you in for this one.'

'I'll have to hurry you, I'm seeing a Mr Bonaparte at two o'clock.'

'Your mother's quite a fox – I'm not surprised you want to shag her.'

'What you made there was what we call a Freudian cock – I mean slip.'

'Deny it all you like, I can tell you fancy me.'

'Sorry, you're not allowed up on the couch.'

'If you feel a bump – that'll be my erection.'

'I'd like to analyse your dreams – but only the filthy ones.'

'Never mind about your childhood.'

'Well, I don't get many eighteen-year-old blondes who try and cure me of their sexual – oh, I've come.'

'You're what we psychiatrists refer to, technically, as a "fruitcake".'

'You lie on the couch, which I've just noticed resembles a giant penis.'

'I think I can diagnose your condition – you're mental.'

'No, no, keep talking – my iPod's playing up.'

'Tell me your sexual hang-ups again, Miss Jones – only more slowly and in time with my right hand. I'll just get some tissues.'

'The good news is that you are perfectly sane. The bad news is that I'm as mad as a hatter.'

'We'll try word association. I'll say a word and you say the first thing that comes into your breasts.'

'OK, I'm going to show you some objects, what do they make you think of? The first one is ... my penis.'

'Well, I've read all of Freud, although admittedly I mean Clement.'

'Sane? You've just paid me £300 for the last hour.'

'You don't have to be mad to come here, but you are.'

23. UNLIKELY THINGS TO HEAR ON A HOLIDAY PROGRAMME (Part 1)

'Frankly, I found the reps' blow jobs were too slurpy and toothy and I won't come again.'

'On tonight's show I'll be visiting a yoga retreat to be annoyed by a lot of neurotic middle-aged women and a single predatory man.'

'I'd been vaccinated against typhoid, but unfortunately John wasn't as well prepared.'

'If you want the holiday that Judith and I enjoyed on this programme then you'll have to be extremely rich.'

'You won't be pestered by local children – they're all at work in the training-shoe factory.'

'Don't make the mistake of smoking in the street – if you're a woman you might just find yourself on the receiving end of death by stoning ... like this ... arrrgghhh ...'

'The locals are all friendly, but not as friendly as our Algerian cameraman who I saw roughly taking Ann from behind on the terrace at 3 a.m. last night.'

'There's loads to do in the hotel, which is lucky as we haven't been allowed out since the coup.'

'What part of "chips" don't you understand, dago?'

'Cocaine is strictly forbidden in Dubai, so you'd best bring your own.'

'You can enjoy a walking holiday in the recently cleared minefields of Mozam-BOOM!'

'We've come to Ibiza to study their culture – but really we've come to look at girls' breasts.'

'Don't worry if your French isn't up to standard, the locals are more than happy for you to point and shout in English.'

'This beautiful hotel with swimming pool is just one of the fantastic places your licence fee is going.'

'For some people, Thailand is just about hot weather, cheap drugs, cheap drinks and easy sex, and I'm one of those people. Let's get down to it!'

'You can find accommodation for as little as £5, but it will be shit.'

'If you're travelling through Europe this summer, remember these three basic rules: the Germans have no sense of humour, the French smell and Greeks are thieves.'

'If you enjoy a bit of "pick your own" you'll love the opium poppy fields of Afghanistan.'

'Things were going from bad to worse as I'd been abducted by rebels and forced to fight against the Revolutionary Guard.'

24. UNLIKELY U.S. IMMIGRATION CARD QUESTIONS (Part 1)

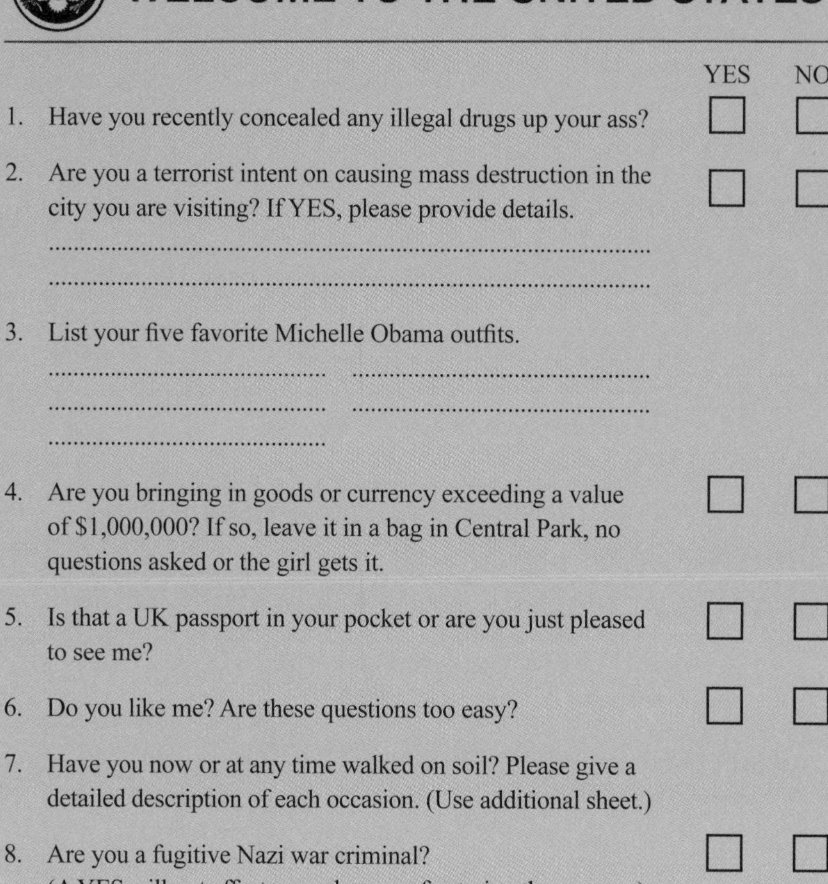

WELCOME TO THE UNITED STATES

		YES	NO
1.	Have you recently concealed any illegal drugs up your ass?	☐	☐
2.	Are you a terrorist intent on causing mass destruction in the city you are visiting? If YES, please provide details.	☐	☐
3.	List your five favorite Michelle Obama outfits.		
4.	Are you bringing in goods or currency exceeding a value of $1,000,000? If so, leave it in a bag in Central Park, no questions asked or the girl gets it.	☐	☐
5.	Is that a UK passport in your pocket or are you just pleased to see me?	☐	☐
6.	Do you like me? Are these questions too easy?	☐	☐
7.	Have you now or at any time walked on soil? Please give a detailed description of each occasion. (Use additional sheet.)		
8.	Are you a fugitive Nazi war criminal? (A YES will not affect your chances of entering the country.)	☐	☐

	YES	NO
9. Which of the cast of *Friends* would you do first?		
10. If you are on a short stay, please give details of hotel and possibly places to eat, bars, shows, tourist destinations and lively nightspots.		
11. Is this the card you were thinking of?	☐	☐
12. Are you traveling with any members of your family? If NO, what are you doing tonight?	☐	☐
13. In your hand luggage do you have any agricultural machinery such as a combine harvester or threshing machine?	☐	☐
14. What is your star sign?		
15. Are you or have you ever been Cat Stevens?	☐	☐
16. Is your job something you do outdoors? Could I do it? Do you wear a uniform? Do you serve the public? Am I getting warm?	☐	☐
17. Are you smuggling in a pig or is that yo mama?	☐	☐
18. Are you here on business, pleasure, or making a sneery, self-indulgent documentary for BBC4?	☐	☐
19. Have you ever taken part in genocide? If NO, how many people have you killed: a)1–10 ☐ b)10–100 ☐ c) lost count but not genocide ☐ d) yeah, OK then, it was genocide. ☐ If d), did they deserve it?	☐	☐

25. WEIRD THINGS TO HAVE TATTOOED ON YOUR ARSE (Part 1)

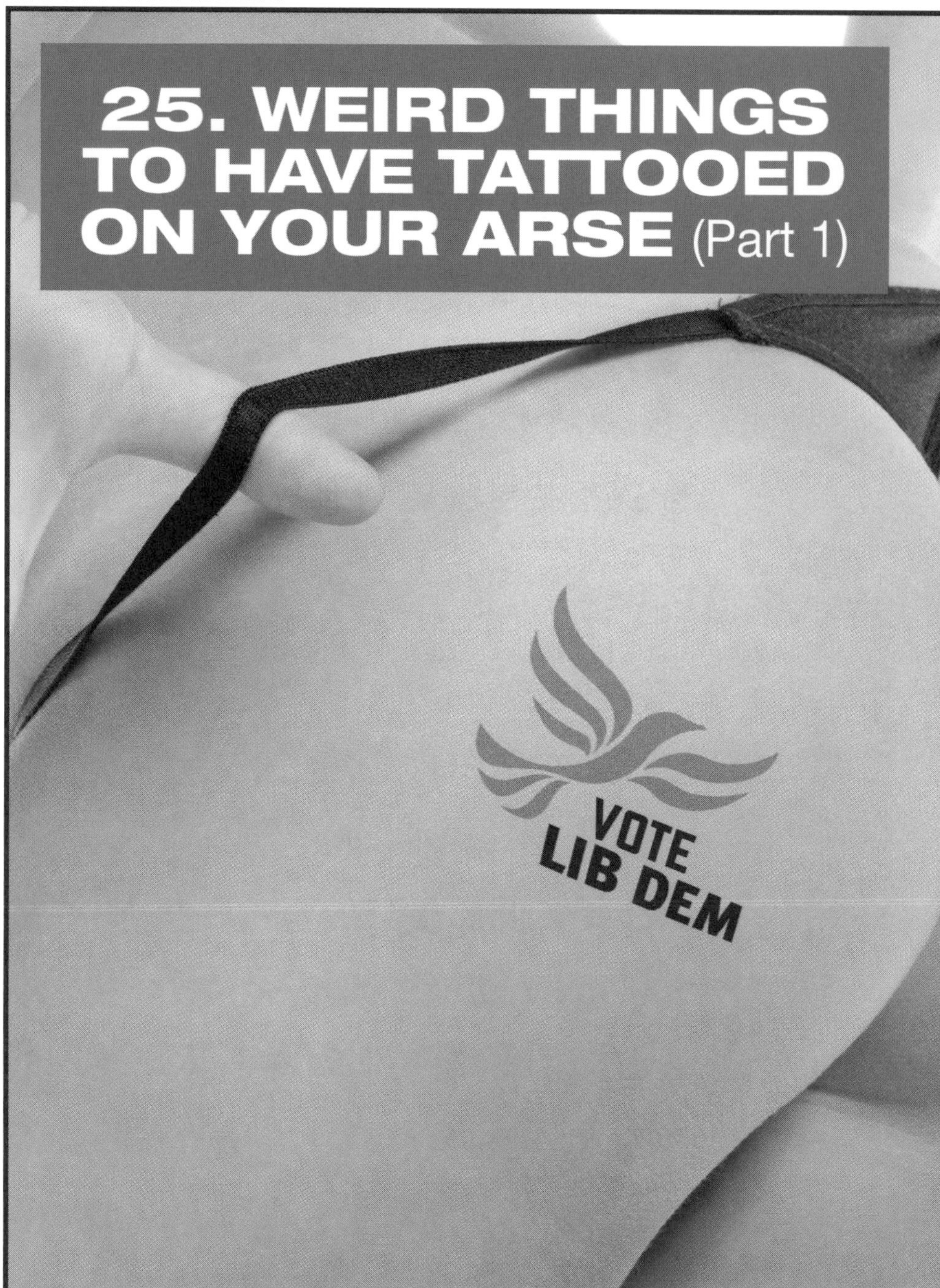

OPEN OTHER END

BEWARE: HAZCHEM

ABANDON HOPE ALL YE WHO ENTER HERE

SUITABLE FOR LONG VEHICLES

THIS CAN BE SEEN FROM SPACE

OW!

IF YOU CAN READ THIS, YOU'RE FAR TOO FUCKING CLOSE

BOY GEORGE RESIDED HERE 1986–1988

WARNING: FALLING SHIT

HONK BEFORE YOU BONK

MAXIMUM WIDTH: 18 INCHES

WISH YOU WERE HERE

GIVE WAY

26. UNLIKELY THINGS TO HEAR FROM A WEATHER FORECASTER

'Today mostly dry with some wet patches, but enough about my trousers.'

'So, Thursday and Friday mild and warm, Saturday an asteroid will hit the Irish Sea and destroy the Earth. That's it from me, bye bye.'

'And as we look … where's Scotland gone? Fuck!'

'And following today's rain of blood, tomorrow doesn't look any better, with a plague of locusts moving in from the west.'

'It'll be shitting it down until Wednesday night.'

'And there's my house where, over the weekend, it'll be raining men. Hallelujah!'

'And for those of you who, like me, had a bet on a white Christmas, there was definitely snow on the roof of the Met Office and I don't care if the bookies make out it wasn't anywhere else, I need that money.'

'What are you watching me for? Just go and look out of the window.'

'Further north it will be wet, moist, damp, juicy, lubricated, oozing, mmm … yes there … mmm, that's it, keep going, sorry, um, showers moving in from the west, should be clear by Tuesday.'

'And if we look at the satellite picture, we can clearly see Iran's nuclear facility, despite what Ahmadinejad says.'

'Clouds here, storms here and, what's this? Oh God, it's . . . oh, I see, someone has just sneezed on the monitor.'

'And as you can see, I can put my head here and completely obscure Yorkshire. If only it were possible to do that in real life.'

'And as for Thursday, if we just have a look at our seaweed, it's mainly dry with occasional showers and 17 degrees.'

'And for the football at Stamford Bridge, bright sunshine, so hopefully that'll mean the fucking blind refs can see them cheating for once.'

'And if we take a quick look at the map I can clearly see we should have taken that turning an hour ago but, oh no, Mr Macho knew the way, he knew better, wouldn't stop and ask, oh no . . .'

'Tomorrow, it'll be bright and sunny . . . BECAUSE I HAVE COMMANDED IT, AND I AM THE GOD OF WEATHER. BOW DOWN, FOOLISH MORTALS!'

'Tomorrow it'll be wetter than my wife's knickers on our wedding night.'

'Thunderbolt and lightning, very very frightening me … Galileo, Galileo Figaro, magnificoooo … '

'And so, as we can see, for the next few days it'll be dark, icy and treacherous, much like the relationship between me and my wife.'

'Moving our satellite pictures on, let's take a look at the weather in Oman. Like any of you give a fuck. What's the betting it's really sunny and dry? Well, bugger me, it is … that useful to all of you in Guildford?'

'And if I put these two clouds closer together and add a snow symbol, see if you think, as I do, that it looks like a fat naked woman bending over a unicorn? Do you see it there, yeah?'

'And tomorrow the Lord shall rain down with the indignation of all his anger and tempest and hailstorms for forty days and forty nights and the lion shall lie down with the lamb.'

'That wet, splashy splashy stuff will be coming down, what's it called again?'

'So there's going to be snow and hail in the north-west on Saturday, possibly some localized flooding. Oh shit. I've got to go to my in-laws' anniversary party in Bolton as well. That's my weekend ruined again.'

'And my forecast is that we'll shit on the Villa, shit on the Villa tonight, 3–1!'

27. UNLIKELY COMPLAINTS TO THE BBC (Part 1)

Dear BBC, what happened to that nice Leslie Grantham? Bring him back. And why no Michael Barrymore? More, please.

Dear BBC, I must complain most strongly about your programme *Points of View* – it gives a platform to gibbering lunatics from the Home Counties. Less, please.

Dear BBC, I once saw a very amusing piece of footage showing the Queen storming away from the throne. Why hasn't it been repeated, over and over again?! Yours, Mr C. Windsor.

Dear BBC, it has also been fifty-five years since you last showed a Coronation – isn't it about time we had another one?! Yours, Mr C. Windsor.

'Stop me or I'll kill again.' Sorry, shouldn't have read that one out.

Dear BBC, given the success of retro shows such as *Strictly Come Dancing*, wouldn't it be a good idea to bring back the good old *Black and White Minstrel Show*?

Dear *Points of View* – are you still on?

I find it most frustrating that just as it gets to a crucial point in *Eastenders*, some drums start playing and the episode's over. It's quite maddening as I then have to watch the next one.

Dear BBC, I write to you but you never write to me.

Dear BBC, what was that music you played over the collapse of the Twin Towers? My friend says it was Showaddywaddy – but I lean towards the Rubettes.

Dear BBC, why don't you pay Jonathan Woss a bigger salawy?

Dear BBC, are you interested in penis enlargement?

Dear BBC, I laughed and laughed and laughed until Huw Edwards stopped reading the news.

Can we please have more programmes with minor celebrities doing everyday things? Yours, Don Estelle from *It Ain't Half Hot Mum*.

Dear BBC, has Eamonn Holmes lost weight? It doesn't look like it to me.

Isn't it time for 4 Poofs and a Piano to get their own show? Yours, The Fat One.

Dear *Points of View*, I have very much enjoyed the latest series of *Anal Adventures*. In fact, I'm watching it now with my trousers round my ankles – here's hoping no one sees me standing outside Dixons.

Dear BBC, shame on you. Last night, you showed a baby seal being clubbed to death, but stopped the film just before the interesting bit. Can you show it, please?

28. UNLIKELY OBITUARIES (Part 2)

IN MEMORIAM

He leaves an enormous hole – in the left-hand side of his head.

... until he was killed by me.

A Tory minister, a high court judge, a military hero and regular churchgoer and now, I feel I can exclusively reveal ... a paedophile.

It is fitting tribute that of the 5,000 people at her memorial service, she had shagged 4,900 of them.

For many years the voice of the speaking clock, his funeral will take place at 5.34 and 18 seconds precisely.

He will be missed, though not, ironically, by the Sudanese firing squad.

Accused of being a fugitive Nazi war criminal, something he vigorously denied all his life from his Argentine villa, 'Green Goebbels'...

He fought the march of time, valiantly but ultimately unsuccessfully. I mean, Christ, the hair plugs, the facelifts and the dyed eyebrows? Liberace aged more gracefully.

He always felt 'twas not a crime, to handle his affairs in rhyme. The life he lived was not in vain, but he died in massive fucking pain.

It is said there are some people who are too good for this world, but Kenny certainly wasn't one of them.

He leaves a wife and four children, much as he did on several occasions during his life.

29. THINGS TO SAY THAT WILL CHANGE THE ATMOSPHERE AT A DINNER PARTY (Part 2)

'Mum, Dad, here's the man I am going to marry … he's called Abu. Abu Hamza.'

'How much money has everyone got in the bank?'

'Cerebral palsy? I thought you were just weird.'

'Whoever left that Stradivarius on the couch, I think one of the kids has just sat on it.'

'I wasn't, I was just stroking the dolphin's stomach.'

'Blindfold taste test: one of these is venison and one is human.'

'So, do you regret divorcing J. K. Rowling?'

'Funny, isn't it? The icing on here tastes like your husband's dick.'

'I think all policemen are Nazis. What do you do? Oh …'

'I always masturbate between the first and second course, don't you?'

'I put on a film to keep the kids quiet – somebody with a deep throat or something.'

'No need to look at your shoes, it's me ... I've shat myself.'

'The last time I was here I was searching your house with the vice squad.'

'Now, before we eat, Steven will choose one of you to be sacrificed to Satan.'

'More lattes? By the way, has anyone seen my breast milk?'

'And now, with her tribute to Shirley Temple, our daughter ...'

'You must be a wonderful teacher, Mrs Jones. Whenever Johnny talks about you, he plays with himself.'

'Mr Andrews, there's a policeman to see you. I say policeman – it's more of an armed response unit.'

'Darling, are these the walnuts Johnny had up his nose?'

'Semen just tastes like humus.'

'Right, I'll go and fetch the fruit bowl, while you lot get your car keys out.'

'You've run out of toilet paper in your loo – so I used a towel.'

30. UNLIKELY THINGS TO READ ON A MOTORWAY SIGN (Part 2)

YOU'RE LATE. GET A MOVE ON. QUICK!

TOM STOPPARD'S BEST WORK IS BEHIND HIM NOW. DISCUSS.

SPEED CAMERAS WITH NO FILM IN AHEAD.

DO THE OPPOSITE OF WHAT THE SIGN SAYS FOR THE NEXT 100 MILES.

TEAR IN SPACE-TIME CONTINUUM AHEAD.

SPEED CAMERAS AHEAD. WOMEN WITH THEIR TITS OUT GET LET OFF.

EDGE OF CLIFF AHEAD. TOO LATE TO SLOW DOWN.

TODAY'S SPEED RESTRICTIONS WERE BROUGHT TO YOU BY POWERGEN.

SIMON SAYS SLOW DOWN AND MOVE TO THE CENTRE LANE.

WATCHING ALL THESE CARS DRIVING PAST MAKES ME HORNY.

IS THAT REALLY THE FASTEST THAT PIECE OF SHIT CAN GO?.

PLACE WHERE THAT BLOKE FROM *'ALLO 'ALLO!* CRASHED AHEAD.

ICE ON ROAD AHEAD. HAVE FUN. FEEL ALIVE. LIVE DANGEROUSLY.

IF YOU DON'T WANT TO KNOW THE RESULT OF TONIGHT'S UEFA CUP SEMI-FINAL, LOOK AWAY NOW.

I AM THE GHOST OF YOUR DRIVING INSTRUCTOR. ONLY YOU CAN READ THIS. I WILL HAVE MY VENGEANCE.

TITS. POO. WANK.
BALLS. OOPS, IS THIS
ON?

31. UNLIKELY COSMETICS COMMERCIALS

'Why? Because I'm incredibly shallow and thick as pig shit.'

'Contains boswellox, which we deliberately made sound a bit rude.'

'Hi, I'm a beauty editor, and people often ask me what my secret is to looking young. I always say, massive amounts of plastic surgery.'

'For proven action against wrinkles, try bathing in the blood of young virgins nightly.'

'Our face cleanser is made with all natural ingredients. In so much as God invented acid.'

'None of our products was tested on animals. We use Filipino children.'

'Buy our mascara or all our lab monkeys will have been blinded for nothing.'

'The Seven Signs of Ageing are: incontinence, grumpiness, a musty smell, saying "Ooh" whenever you sit down, lack of knowledge of popular music, shopping in shops selling tweed and driving in the middle lane bang on the speed limit.'

'Hi, I'm a beauty editor, and people are always asking me what my secret is. Well, I murdered my first husband.'

'Nivea feels good on my face and even better on my balls.'

'This woman looks fantastic – but she's a model. You're not.'

'That's me three months ago when I was just a pre-op transsexual.'

'My hair used to be curly and tight, now my pubes are long and luxuriant like I've just stepped out of a salon.'

'After just one application, my blackheads are erupting like landmines.'

'People often ask how I keep my gash looking so neat and moist ...'

'Why not consolidate all your looks into one easily manageable face?'

'Try our face pack, with avocado oil and citrus extract. Or use it as a tasty dip.'

(*To be read out quickly*) 'This advert may be thoroughly misleading, this product does not work at all and may burn your face off.'

'Our lipstick looks great on rabbits – think how good it'll look on you!'

'Fake Tan – for when you just *have* to look like an Oompa Loompa.'

'Superdrug – because, although you may be worth it, you don't have any money.'

'I'm Heather Mills and I'm here to talk to you about having smooth legs with Ronseal Quick Drying Woodstain.'

32. BAD *QUESTION TIME* QUESTIONS (Part 1)

'Can I just illustrate that I haven't understood anything anyone has said on this topic?'

'I'd like to ask Ruth Kelly if she's a boy or a girl.'

'Does anyone want to shag me?'

'Can I paraphrase what the man here just said, but get it a bit wrong?'

'I'd like to ask the panel if they've got a trite but populist answer to this question that will guarantee a round of applause?'

'I'd like to ask, are Lib Dems becoming forgettable? That question to, er, whatsisname at the end, next to the Tory.'

'Just time for one last question. Yes, you sir.'

'Me? I would like to ask the panel if they feel that last questions are sometimes a bit of an anti-climax?'

'Do the panel think David Dimbleby should be replaced?'

'Does this blouse go with these trousers?'

'I'd like to ask the panel: what do they think about when they're knocking one out?'

'If the panel were a fish what fish would they be, and why? That question to number one.'

'I'd like to ask the Prime Minister what he would do if he wasn't such a useless twat.'

'Another question – yes, you Sir, the absurdly gay man at the back.'

'What are your favourite colours?'

'I'd like to ask the panel: are they aware the Carling Cup highlights are on the other side?'

'Welcome to the programme that looks like democracy but is really cheap entertainment for the angry.'

'Welcome to a *Question Time* special, where all the guests are naked.'

'Which member of the audience would like to have their intelligence insulted next?'

33. UNLIKELY PROPERTY MAGAZINE ADVERTS (Part 2)

• FOR SALE

Beautiful North London villa – great potential if you can get rid of any of the 49 Kosovan gangsters currently squatting there.

FOR SALE: straw house and stick house. Both in need of renovation. Apply brick house. No wolves.

Deceptively large bungalow with extensive sewing and lepidoptery facilities, large ground-floor pit, would suit *Silence of the Lambs* fan.

Three foot square, would suit short and thin person.

Bijou cottage with views of town abbatoir.

Paedophile's dream: luxury apartment with unspoilt view of playground of local primary school and situated within a three-minute walk of nearest sweet shop.

At the centre of a busy community – of rock-wielding hoodies.

ACT NOW. Before they find out I didn't get planning permission.

Loud, pink, flamboyant apartment, ideal for poofs.

'Get back to nature' with wonderful opportunity to acquire unique 4,000 square foot apartment with no walls or roof.

A stunning, unspoilt, remote location ideal for someone on the run from the police or who will never need post, shopping or assistance from the emergency services.

The wonderfully appointed lounge has beautiful red spattered wall decoration and floors and a charming chalk outline human figure in the middle of the floor.

Wake up under the stars with this spacious Thameside two-zip luxury one-tog sleeping bag, within easy reach of Waterloo Bridge. Oil-fired central heating provided via rusty can with holes in.

Deluxe ground-floor flat, own patio, garden and Grade II listed plague pit.

They say it's uninhabitable, come and prove them wrong.

House bought as seen with fixtures, fittings and murder trial evidence.

Beautiful rural property with own swimming pool (for a month every year when the river bursts).

Priced for quick sale as owner needs to flee country.

LOT FOR SALE: Salisbury Plain. Located in the middle of the sought-after Firing Range area.

34. CARDS YOU NEVER SEE IN A NEWSAGENT'S WINDOW (Part 2)

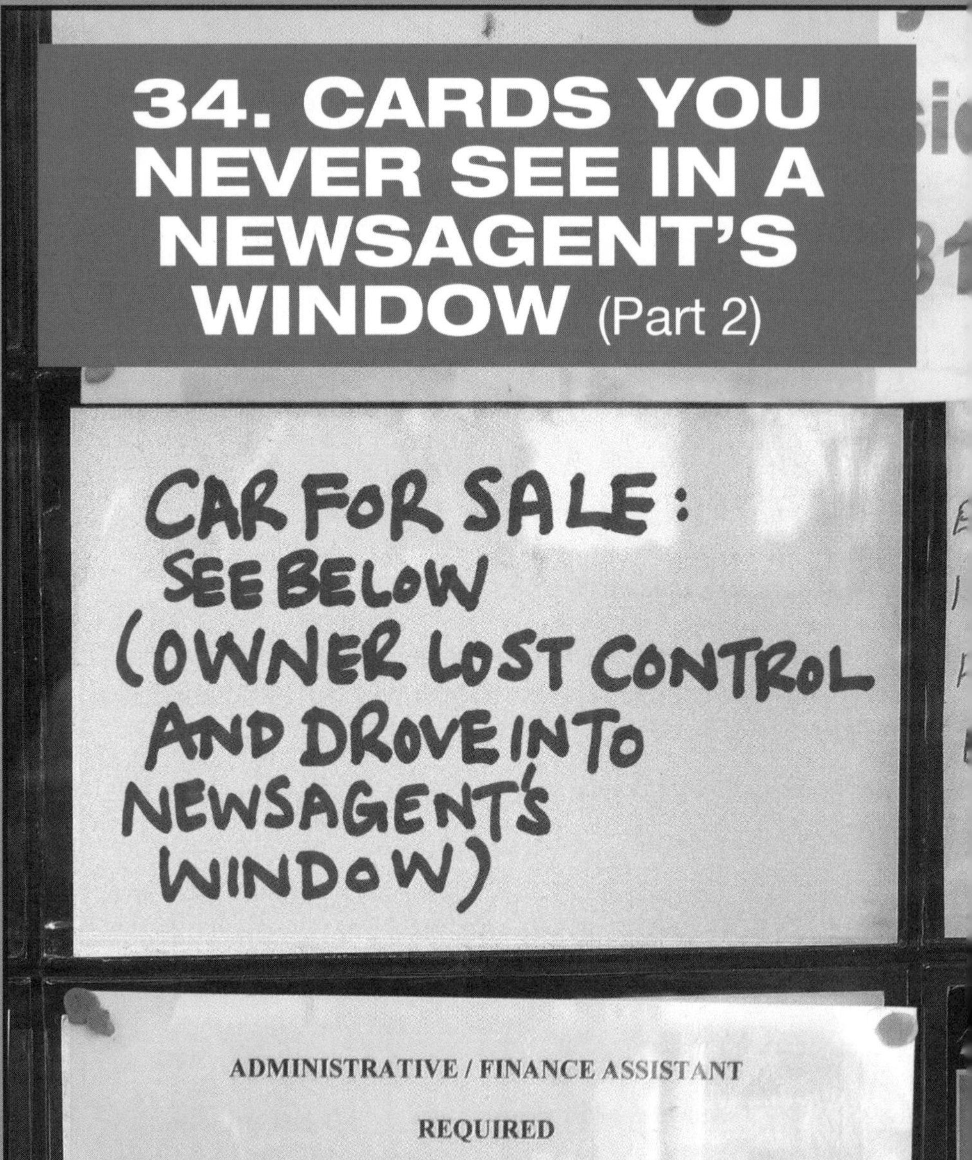

CAR FOR SALE:
SEE BELOW
(OWNER LOST CONTROL
AND DROVE INTO
NEWSAGENT'S
WINDOW)

ADMINISTRATIVE / FINANCE ASSISTANT
REQUIRED
RS PER WEEK
LY MON – FRI
am to 2pm

Man With Van

ILLEGAL IMMIGRANTS WANTED FOR POTENTIALLY LETHAL AGRICULTURAL JOBS. MEET ME HERE 3.30 A.M. NEXT TUESDAY.

I AM GENUINELY NEW IN TOWN AND INTERESTED IN MAKING FRIENDS AND SEEING THE SIGHTS. NB: I'M A PRE-OP TRANSSEXUAL WHO IS A PROSTITUTE. RING THIS NUMBER.

ODD BLOW JOB MAN – NO KNOB TOO SMALL.

CHURCH FATE: PROBABLY EVENTUAL CLOSURE DUE TO APATHY AND DEVELOPMENT INTO LUXURY FLATS ...

FOUND: PUPPY IN LARGE, DAMP SACK FULL OF STONES. BEGINNING TO SMELL.

ROOM TO RENT IN LARGE CENTRAL LONDON TOWNHOUSE WITH THREE LESBIAN NYMPHOMANIAC SUPERMODELS, £50 PW.

CAR FOR SALE. RED ONE WITH FOUR WHEELS. ONE LADY OWNER.

BABYSITTER, 17, VERY MATURE, £5 AN HOUR AND A 'LIFT HOME', IF YOU KNOW WHAT I MEAN.

VILLAGE WEIRDO AVAILABLE FOR HOME VISITS, CHILDREN'S PARTIES AND BUS-SHELTER LOITERING. CONTACT VIA INTERNET 24/7.

VILLAGE BIKE FOR SALE. GOES WELL. NEEDS OILING. BUYER COLLECTS. ANSWERS TO THE NAME OF 'GILLIAN'.

ME: 45, 6FT, SINGLE PROFESSIONAL, GSOH, LOVES GARDENING, CLASSICAL MUSIC AND TELLING PEOPLE ABOUT MYSELF.

35. THINGS YOU WOULDN'T HEAR ON CHILDREN'S TV (Part 1)

'Hello, I'm Uncle Pockets, come on Vanessa, come and have a delve, see what I've got, keep going, deeper, that's it, keep feeling around there, go on ...'

'This story was sent in by Jemima White, aged seven, it's very good, so good in fact that we think your mum wrote it, so you're not having the prize. Let that be a lesson to Mrs pushy fucking White.'

'This week's episode of *High School Musical* has had to be cancelled as one of the pupils has gone on the rampage with a gun.'

'And on today's episode of *Clifford the Big Red Dog*, Clifford does an enormous shit in the garden.'

'Next up is *Balamory*. If you don't want to be singing the theme tune all day long, turn over now.'

'So you smear them with honey like so, and ... let's give it a go ... Shep, come here boy.'

'In this week's episode of *Camberwick Green*, Pugh, Pugh, Barney McGrew, Cuthbert, Dibble and Grub come under a hail of bottles as they attend a car fire on a council estate.'

'In this week's edition of *Bob the Builder*, Bob is replaced by

Bogodan the builder from Poland.'

'You'll need a pair of scissors for this – so grab some while your mum's not looking.'

'I'm afraid the *Blue Peter* golden retriever has died – it was flattened by a ten-ton truck while shagging a spaniel on the hard shoulder.'

'Another way to make pocket money is to film your parents having sex and then post it on the Internet.'

'Oh, no, Bob the Builder – here's Vern the VAT Man!'

'Hi kids, retired and unemployed people!'

'Hi kids, no one presents kids' telly because they want to.'

'Sadly, Fireman Sam's breathing equipment was faulty ...'

'Here comes Gordon, the big homosexual engine ... with a tender behind.'

'This is my last *Play School* because my bastard ex-boyfriend has posted a video of me snorting coke and giving him a blow job on the Internet. Bye-bye!'

'"It's not true about them having nine lives, then," said Pat, having accidentally reversed over Jess ...'

'You'll need grown-ups to help you cut this picture out – as you won't be allowed to buy the porn mag yourself.'

'So, Scooby, the janitor wasn't pretending to be a mummy, he just had terrible burns from a recent accident.'

36. UNLIKELY NATIONAL HOLIDAYS

ROLF HARRIS ARRIVAL IN BRITAIN DAY

STOP BLOODY MOANING DAY

NATIONAL HAEMORRHOID WEEK

PMT DAY OF ANGER

DIANA & DODI DAY

MANIC MONDAY

RAINY DAY

FESTIVAL OF SHITS

SUNDAY BLOODY SUNDAY

NEW SERIES OF GRAHAM NORTON AWARENESS WEEK

VICTORY IN IRAQ DAY

SADDAM: 'WE GOT HIM' DAY

RAY STUBBS'S FIRST *FOOTBALL FOCUS* DAY

BLOW JOB THURSDAY

WHAT A GAY DAY

HALF-PRICE DAY AT DFS

DARREN DAY

37. UNLIKELY SMALL ADS (Part 1)

FOR SALE

Bloody hunting knife for sale. Make me an offer, quickly.

Half a cold latte for sale, only bought yesterday, would benefit from heating.

£20 – I wasn't born yesterday, but this baby was.

ERRATA: Thank you for the enquiries for the catamaran for sale for £10 yesterday. Advert should have read: cat and meringue for sale, £10.

Gobstopper for sale, first three colours sucked off for you.

FOR SALE: litre of petrol, £10. Buyer collects.

Hitler diaries for sale. The perfect 2010 organizer for the Nazi in your life.

Pre-op transsexual – which I suppose translates as 'bloke'.

Animal lover and DIY enthusiast seeks to sell three-legged elephant plus umbrella stand.

Viagra wanted – unable to locate on the Internet anywhere.

Fancy a massage? I'm big and busty – with man boobs and a beer gut.

38. UNLIKELY LINES FROM A SCI-FI FILM
(Part 2)

'INLAND REVENUE, MR JEDI – IT'S ABOUT YOUR RETURN.'

'THIS IS MY WATCH, IT IS CALLED A "DIGITAL".'

'HELLO, BIG BOY. SO, WHY DO THEY CALL YOU "CHEWY"?'

'LOOK, DARTH, WE'VE JUST COME 4,000 LIGHT YEARS. ARE YOU SURE YOU LEFT THE IRON ON?'

'I HAVE TWO HEARTS AND FOURTEEN ANUSES.'

'CAPTAIN, I TELEPORTED DOWN TO THE PLANET BUT I SEEM TO HAVE LOST MY COCK IN THE PROCESS.'

'THERE HE IS, OFFICER. IT'S THAT GUY FROM THE FUTURE BETTING ON THE 3.30 AT HAYDOCK AGAIN.'

'SCOTTY, YOU'VE UNDERESTIMATED THE GRAVITY AGAIN. I THINK I'VE BROKEN MY NOSE ON THE PAVEMENT.'

'ILL-THOUGHT OUT, AND FRANKLY DREADFUL PREQUEL, THIS IS.'

'EARTHLINGS, YOUR WEAPONS ARE USELESS AGAINST US – THEY'RE BRITISH-MADE.'

'MY MOTHER IS FROM EARTH BUT MY FATHER IS A VULCAN, WHICH IS WHY I'M CIRCUMCISED.'

'APPARENTLY CHEKHOV HAS GOT THREE SISTERS, IF YOU KNOW WHAT I MEAN.'

'PRINCESS LEIA, YOU SAY YOU'VE NEVER BEEN TO EARTH, YET YOU HAVE HAIR LIKE A DANISH PASTRY.'

'I'VE JUST SEEN C3PO NUTS AND BOLTS DEEP IN R2D2.'

'THE DILITHIUM CRYSTALS, CAPTAIN – THEY'RE ABSOLUTELY FINE.'

'WE'VE BEEN HIT BY THE KLINGONS – EVERYONE WOBBLE FROM LEFT TO RIGHT.'

'CAPTAIN'S LOG: BLAH BLAH, FIVE-YEAR MISSION, YADDA YADDA ...'

'GORDON'S ALIVE, BUT IT'S NOT LOOKING GOOD.'

'GORDON'S HAD A STROKE!'

'GORDON'S IN A PERMANENT VEGETATIVE STATE.'

39. UNLIKELY THINGS TO FIND WRITTEN ON TOILET PAPER PACKAGING (Part 2)

Degradable packaging

Chicken and Mushroom flavour

Because you're worth it

Feels like having your arse licked by a big slobbery dog

No salt added

Tested on animals

Go back to school with new 'Tracing Paper' range, or see what you're doing with new Bacofoil Bog Roll

Serving suggestion

Do not operate heavy machinery when using

Smoking can damage your health

Does not contain nuts

Will explode on contact with water

Recycled – that's why it's such a funny colour

New Anal Excel Phallic, clean your arse and be rogered at the same time

Reusable

Just add water

You can use as many cute puppies as you like, but all this does is wipe shit out of the crack of your arse

40. THINGS THAT WOULD RUIN A MEAL IN A RESTAURANT (Part 2)

'Would Sir like to suck my knob now?

'No, that isn't beetroot on your salad, Sir, it's the chef's blood.'

'Sorry it's a bit undercooked, the chef is normally the washer-upper.'

'Three banoffee pies – I'll bring them after I've had a dump.'

[Fill-in questionnaire:] Do *you* think we're unhygenic?

'The smelly old tramp on the next table sent over this bottle of meths for you.'

'Fillet of battery-farmed, bolt-killed Norfolk chicken.'

'Excuse me, ladies, I was just listening to your conversation, I wonder if you'd mind me silently masturbating?'

'We need the table back by 9 p.m., it's 8.54 now, so … two bananas and the bill?'

'No, it isn't sunburn, it's psoriasis.'

'Can anyone eating the lychee salad just stop for a moment? The chef has lost his false eye.'

'No, Sir, it's pig rectum, stuffed with goat's jizz on a bed of horse shit. We don't sell many; in fact, you're the first person to order it.'

'It can be lethal if the chef doesn't cook it exactly right.'

'Unscrew my hand, I've got a bottle-opener attachment.'

'Yes, I'll heat it up, down my trousers.'

'Waiter, have you got frog's legs?'
'No, I'm disabled, you c**t.'

'The only table left is very close to the toilets.
In fact it's in a cubicle.'

'Most amusing waiter joke, Sir – remind me which soup you were having?'

'Sweetcorn and beetroot risotto – you'll be seeing that in every one of your shits this week, Sir.'

'It is self service. Chef, release the goose!'

'We'll have to sit you with the German naturist party.'

'We'll keep you under observation for an hour or so after you've finished and then you can go.'

41. UNLIKELY THINGS TO HEAR IN A WAR FILM (Part 2)

'MISSION ACCOMPLISHED, SIR – AS ORDERED, I'VE BEEN SHAVING RYAN'S PRIVATES.'

'PLATOON! PHASERS SET TO "STUN".'

'TOMORROW IS THE BIG PUSH, MEN, AND I'VE EATEN A WHOLE BOX OF LAXATIVES IN PREPARATION.'

'OOH, I'VE RUINED THESE TROUSERS.'

'WE'RE OUT OF GUNS, PERKINS, USE THIS FRISBEE.'

'WATCH OUT, SERGEANT, HE'S WEARING A RUCKSACK.'

'I'LL START THE TUNNEL HERE, CAVENDISH, YOU START THE COVERED WALKWAY FROM THE FOURTH FLOOR.'

'ROMMEL, I DIDN'T EXPECT TO SEE YOU IN HERE AND EATING A FAMILY BUCKET.'

'I'M WORRIED – NOW I'VE SHOWN YOU A PHOTOGRAPH OF MY WIFE AND MY FARM BACK HOME, I DON'T THINK I'M GOING TO MAKE IT.'

'OK, MEN, LISTEN, THIS IS WHAT WE'RE GOING TO DO: CLIMB THAT WALL, RUN ALONG THE TOP, CROSS THE GREASY BRIDGE, SHIMMY UP NELSON AND RING THE BELL. THE GERMANS WILL BE THROWING WET SPONGES AT YOU.'

'YOU MIGHT BE ON TO SOMETHING HERE, BARNES WALLIS - THE BOUNCING PLANE, YOU SAY?'

'GET ME A SHOT OF MORPHINE. I HAVEN'T BEEN INJURED, I JUST REALLY WANT A SHOT OF MORPHINE.'

'EXCUSE ME, SERGEANT - THIS STRETCH OF THE WESTERN FRONT ISN'T NEARLY AS QUIET AS I WAS LED TO BELIEVE.'

'VON RYAN'S EXPRESS WOULD LIKE TO APOLOGIZE FOR THE LATE RUNNING OF THIS TRAIN.'

'I THINK JERRY IS HIDING BEHIND THAT BUILDING. FUCK KNOWS WHERE TOM IS, THOUGH.'

'SO, THE BULLET BOUNCED OFF THE CIGARETTE CASE IN HIS BREAST POCKET AND RICOCHETED STRAIGHT UP INTO HIS BRAIN.'

'I'M WORRIED ABOUT OUR FORGER'S EYESIGHT. HE'S JUST MADE ME THIS DEUTSCHE PISSPORT.'

'YOU GET IN THE PLANE AND WE'LL CATAPULT IT OFF THE ROOF. WHILE THE GERMANS ARE PICKING UP THE PIECES OF YOUR BODY, WE'LL NIP OVER THE FENCE.'

42. BAD THINGS TO SAY AT A WEDDING (Part 1)

'Let's have one of the bride flashing her garter … now one with her knickers on.'

'The next hymn was chosen by the bride, although it's clearly not about her – "All Things Bright and Beautiful".'

'If we could dim the lights, I will now spend twenty minutes trying and failing to set up an anticlimactic slide and PowerPoint show …'

'When you throw rice, you're meant to take it out of the bag.'

'Till WHAT us do part?'

'You may kiss the bride, she love you long time.'

'We've done the other group photos – now for everybody who's slept with the bride.'

'Till death or a canoe fraud do us part.'

'Which one of you has the cock rings?'

'We've done an exclusive for the photos – with *Razzle* magazine.'

'Congratulations, Mr George, you may now stalk the bride.'

'I've been asked not to talk about the stag do, not by the groom, but by the embarrassed teenage boy he shagged.'

'If anyone knows any reason why they should not be wed – well, I'll start the ball rolling.'

'Go on – if I shag you, I'll have done the full set of bridesmaids.'

'I've never seen a bride looking as lovely as Jennifer does today – and believe me, I've seen some pretty strong contenders on hotbridesbeggingforaction.com.'

'Since you ask, this isn't the *first* time I've met your sister.'

SHAGGER 4 BIFFER

43. UNSUCCESSFUL JOB APPLICATIONS

I am a team player – in fact, I'm probably the single best team player in the country.

You must hire me, before I kill again!

I am conscientious, hardworking, tenacious, etc., etc.

I understand you're an Equal Opportunities employer, so I bet you've got some cracking birds in the office.

I have a lot of experience of charity work – I'm one of those annoying people on the street with sweatshirts and clipboards.

Dear Conservative Selection Committee, I didn't go to Eton – does it matter?

I am highly computer literate, with an excellent working knowledge of ZX Spectrum, Casio FX21, and Amstrad skills.

Having been on ten previous missions, I bring a wealth of experience to the art of suicide bombing.

In my free time, I enjoy being a scout leader, a choirmaster and going on the Internet.

My greatest achievement? Level 37, Super Mario Galaxy Racer.

I have a Duke of Edinburgh award – I've insulted a lot of Chinese people.

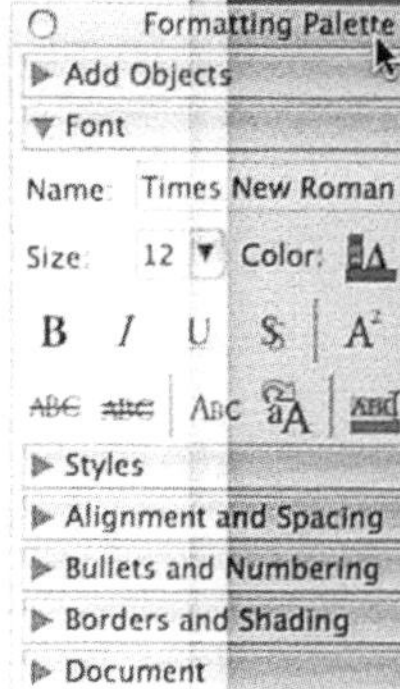

Despite my lack of medical qualifications, I feel that gynaecology is a calling.

Full-time catering experience, 1987–2005 Wormwood Scrubs kitchen trustee, E Wing.

Please consult my CV – or Cunnilingus Vitae.

I'm a black lesbian in a wheelchair – how many more boxes do you want to tick?

I love to work closely with animals – you may have seen some of my work on the Internet.

I believe I should be given this job and all the major responsibilities it entails, because, you never know, it could be a laugh.

I'd like to join the army because there's nothing I like more than the sight of other men in uniform.

Dear Mrs Johnson, I am 18, Swedish and beautiful and I'd love to work as an au pair for you and Boris.

Hobbies: Wining and dining, dancing, narcotics, trawling motorway service stations, taxidermy.

I worked very hard to get to the top of my father's company.

... and here's a link to photos of me throwing up on Facebook.

I have a full array of computer skills. Look at the way I've Photoshopped your face into this highly unusual threesome.

44. UNLIKLEY THINGS TO HEAR ON THE *ANTIQUES ROADSHOW*

'Well, Sir, it's absolutely incredible, I have to admit I've rarely seen one as large or well preserved as that, but if you could put it away now and show us your antique?'

'Today you join us at the Winston Silcott Youth Centre in Brixton.'

'Now then, now then, these are the Duchess's clothes, kept them in my wardrobe, you see.'

'It's been in the family about errm ... four minutes ... I saw it sticking out of that old man's rucksack.'

'What you have here is an old Victorian sex toy. Do you still use it?'

'It's fucking worth more than that.'

'I'm not sure they had GuitarHero in the eighteenth century.'

'It looks like a Victorian carriage clock but I'm just going to look it up on Google.'

'Yes, it's an original Rembrandt, but it's probably only worth, um, a fiver. Would you, er, like me to take it off your hands?'

'There's loads more where this come from, mate, mum's the word.'

'Yes, I got given this ceremonial sceptre when I became Prince of Wales. It's been in the family since the War of the Roses, what's it worth? I need the cash, the organic biscuit market's gone tits up.'

'These are the clothes from my mother – I'm telling him, I'm telling him, mother!'

'Well, let's have a look at him ... I think he's worth quite a lot of money, but all I know is he's very old, not in very good condition and is married to Catherine Zeta Jones.'

'I actually got it from my father, along with chlamydia.'

'And if you notice this little insignia down here on the base ... it says IKEA.'

'It's a beautiful piece, now how come a young hoodie like you got hold of it, sonny?'

'Cut the crap, mate, how much is it worth and do you want to buy it? I've got other people interested.'

'Its origins are uncertain but it's been with the same family for more than twenty years – a bit like Prince Harry.'

'What a piece of shit.'

'Yes, it's an urn containing the ashes of Arthur Negus.'

'Oh dear, you ain't paid us this month Miss Bruce, have you? That's a nice vase, be a real shame if someone dropped it. Oopsy daisy, I'm feeling clumsy, oh dear, oh dear.'

45. UNNERVING THINGS TO HEAR IN A MEDICAL EXAM (Part 2)

'If you could just pop your clothes off in time to this music and look into the camera.'

'I'm just looking into your ear and ... what's this? A pound coin? A bunch of flowers? A dove?'

'Your penis is a perfectly normal size ... if you were a vole.'

'Now, what seems to be the ... fucking hell!'

'It can't be what it looks like – you can only get it if you've shagged a dog ... why are you crying?'

'Just one moment, Mr Johnson – Hello, is that Channel 5? I think I've got another documentary idea for you.'

'Eurgh, I'm not touching that.'

'We are going to test your reflexes and practise my knife-throwing act at the same time.'

'There's something wrong with your clitoris but I can't quite put my finger on it.'

'Brian, you've got to come and see this!'

'I'm afraid it's bad news, you've got ... oh hang on, there's the phone, can I take this? Yes, hi, this won't take long will it? Only I'm with a patient and she might not make it to the end of this call.'

'I'm afraid you've got Parkinson's Disease. This means you'll start interviewing people ... only kidding, no, you've got Parkinson's.'

'OK, your breasts look fine. Would you like to see my cock in exchange?'

'Can I get a picture? I'm doing a book on freaks.'

'Everyone ... clear! I've just farted.'

'You need to take a spoonful of semen every day – 4 p.m. is best for me...'

'I'm going to need a second opinion, because I'm not actually a doctor.'

46. UNLIKELY THINGS TO READ ON A MOTORWAY SIGN (Part 3)

SOME OF THE FOLLOWING SIGNS CONTAIN STRONG LANGUAGE AND SCENES OF A SEXUAL NATURE.

THERE MAY BE TROUBLE AHEAD. PREPARE TO FACE MUSIC AND DANCE.

HUGE FATAL CRASH HERE ON 25 APRIL. LET ME KNOW IF YOU CAN MAKE IT.

LAST CHANCE TO MISS EXIT FOR FIVE MILES.

WELCOME TO CONE WORLD THEME PARK.

EIGHT-LANE MOTORWAY WIDENING PROJECT AHEAD – FIVE LANES SHUT.

CAUTION: CRACKS IN BUILDERS' ARSES AHEAD.

SERVICES 1 MILE – CLEAN SERVICES 25 MILES.

VELCOME TO ZE AUTOBAHN – PLEAZ DRIVE LIKE EIN LUNATIC.

TEDIOUS GAME OF I SPY, NEXT 100 MILES.

EXPECT DELAYS. DON'T KNOW WHERE OR WHEN, JUST EXPECT THEM.

DUE TO LACK OF CAT'S EYES, BEWARE DWARVES PEEPING OUT OF HOLES, WEARING SILVER CONTACT LENSES.

WORRYING TYRE FRAGMENTS – NEXT 200 YARDS.

NICE COMBOVER,
SLAPHEAD
TAGLIE GRANDI
A1
11

47. UNLIKELY THINGS TO HEAR ON A HOLIDAY PROGRAMME (Part 2)

'If, like me, you are just here for the sex tourism, wander down into the docks area around 9 p.m. to 4 a.m. any night.'

'You can actually have a pretty cheap holiday if you use a bit of nouse – for instance, you can get street children to carry you around in a sedan chair for a whole day, for just a couple of dollars.'

'If you're going to try and smuggle back drugs, shoving them up your rectum is probably the best bet.'

'The Rhine cruise is enjoyable, but be warned: it is full of Germans.'

'I'm Judith Chalmers and you may need to adjust the colour on your set.'

'... is one of the city's best restaurants and you can order most things without worrying you'll be puking and shitting like a two-way blender with no lid.'

'Don't drink the water and try not to get mugged – but once you're out of the UK you should be fine.'

'If you don't like people of other colours, then another option is the exclusive resort of Cape Blanco about fifty miles from here.'

'France is a country rich in culture, spoilt only by its people.'

'I lay there naked and warm until I was put back in economy class.'

'I'm lying here with a very large cocktail inside me ... sorry, with a very large cocktail waiter inside me.'

'I'm standing in front of Delhi's newest big attraction, the Network Rail Call Centre.'

'The best thing about this country is the people. They all look so funny, don't they?'

'Tell the flight crew you've got a bomb in your luggage – there's nothing they like more than a good joke.'

'I'm afraid this is an economy flight, we don't have toilets – you'll have to shit in your seat.'

'Here's a tip if you're going to Faliraki – by mid season 90 per cent of the holiday reps will have herpes.'

'There are loads of activities here, which is just as well, as after a few problems at customs I haven't been able to sit down for four days.'

48. UNLIKELY U.S. IMMIGRATION CARD QUESTIONS (Part 2)

WELCOME TO THE UNITED STATES

YES NO

1. How much bigger and stronger than your country is America? ....

2. Are you here on:
   a) business ☐ b) holiday ☐ c) working holiday ☐
   d) a trip where you are meant to be working where it's more like a holiday ☐
   e) a holiday where you may as well be in work you're getting that many phone calls ☐
   f) jihad ☐

3. Were you ever a member of the Communist party? Have you met Brezhnev? If YES, what was he like? .... ☐ ☐

4. Who was the best Doctor Who? ....

5. Where were you on September 11, 2001? Give details. (If answer includes the phrase: 'Trying to board a plane with weapons and a copy of the Koran,' please go directly to question overleaf.) .... ☐ ☐

6. Would you ever wear brown shoes with black trousers? ☐ ☐

7. Please list all US states in order of GDP. (Use additional sheet.)

8. Are you part of the Axis of Evil? ☐ ☐

	YES	NO
9. Can you write that again? I just love your accent		
10. How do you pronounce the word aluminum? Your entry depends on this.		
11. Are you from England? Do you know my friend John? He lives there.	☐	☐
12. Did you kill Trotsky?	☐	☐
13. Only recently can US foreign policy be said to have stepped out of the shadow cast by the Vietnam war. Discuss.		
14. Are you looking at my girlfriend?	☐	☐
15. Complete this sentence in ten words or less to win a prize: 'I have always wanted to visit America because ....'		
16. How was your flight? What did you have for your tea?		
17. Are you carrying more than £10,000 in cash? Giz a bit.	☐	☐
18. When did you last use the toilet? Well, why didn't you go before you left?		
19. Please fill in this card with stickers of US presidents. We've started you off with a free Bill Clinton, Gerald Ford and Grover Cleveland.		
20. Have you recently visited Canada? Shit, isn't it?	☐	☐
21. Are you the head of your household or is it your missus who wears the trousers?	☐	☐
22. Do you know where Amelia Earhart is?	☐	☐

49. UNLIKELY LINES FROM A POLITICAL BIOGRAPHY

We had to leave Downing Street in a hurry that night, because the body in the boot was beginning to smell. A hard night's digging lay ahead of us. 'This is no job for a Cabinet minister,' I said. He laughed, picked up the shovel and spat on his hands.

'What ho, Jeeves! Appoint Gussie Fink-Nottle as my head of security,' said Boris.

Silently, I withdrew from my panting secretary, zipped up me trousers and bit into a nearby sausage roll.

'The Conservatives are fuck all,' I thought, as my fist sank into the doughy nose of David Cameron and my foot sprang into the boyish crotch of George Osbourne.

The scent and smoke and sweat of a negotiating chamber are nauseating at three in the morning, thought Ban Ki Moon.

I am an invisible man, but that's inevitable when you are Shadow Agriculture Minister.

Our eyes met across the Mansion House table. He was in a daring lounge suit, standing out amongst the white tie and stiffness. He winked and seemed to do a funny breathing thing with his mouth. I could tell he wanted me, so I went over and asked his name. 'Brown, Gordon Brown,' he said, breathily.

THIS IS GEORGE BUSH. LOOK. PRESIDENT. LOOK. WAR. OOOH. PRETZEL. LOOK. THE END.

As the wife, spouse, partner, confidante, soul mate and motivator of Tony Blair, I never expected, supposed, considered, guessed, that one day a book publishing company would ask, request, cajole, persuade, force me to write a book, volume, autobiography, memoir, but they said they'd pay by the word.

I Shot JFK and Other Hunting Accidents by Dick Cheney

'Your Highness, it's done,' I said, and turned away from the tunnel and into the dark Parisian night, throwing my mobile and the blinding flashlight into the Seine.

'You're more than just a great Chancellor,' said the Prime Minister. Suddenly, he was on top of me and I felt his mouth against mine.

In my case, MP also stood for massive paedophile.

Clare Short - nah, Harriet Harman - possibly if she didn't speak, Hazel Blears - filthy, Jacqui Smith - phwoar! Caroline Flint - tasty, but like a bag of potatoes in the sack.

it wuzzz nt eezie to mayke itt two the top wiv me lurnin diffficulltyes

Call me Prescott.

Vlad Putin and the Prisoner of Azerbaijan: Chapter Two.

50. WEIRD THINGS TO HAVE TATTOOED ON YOUR ARSE (Part 2)

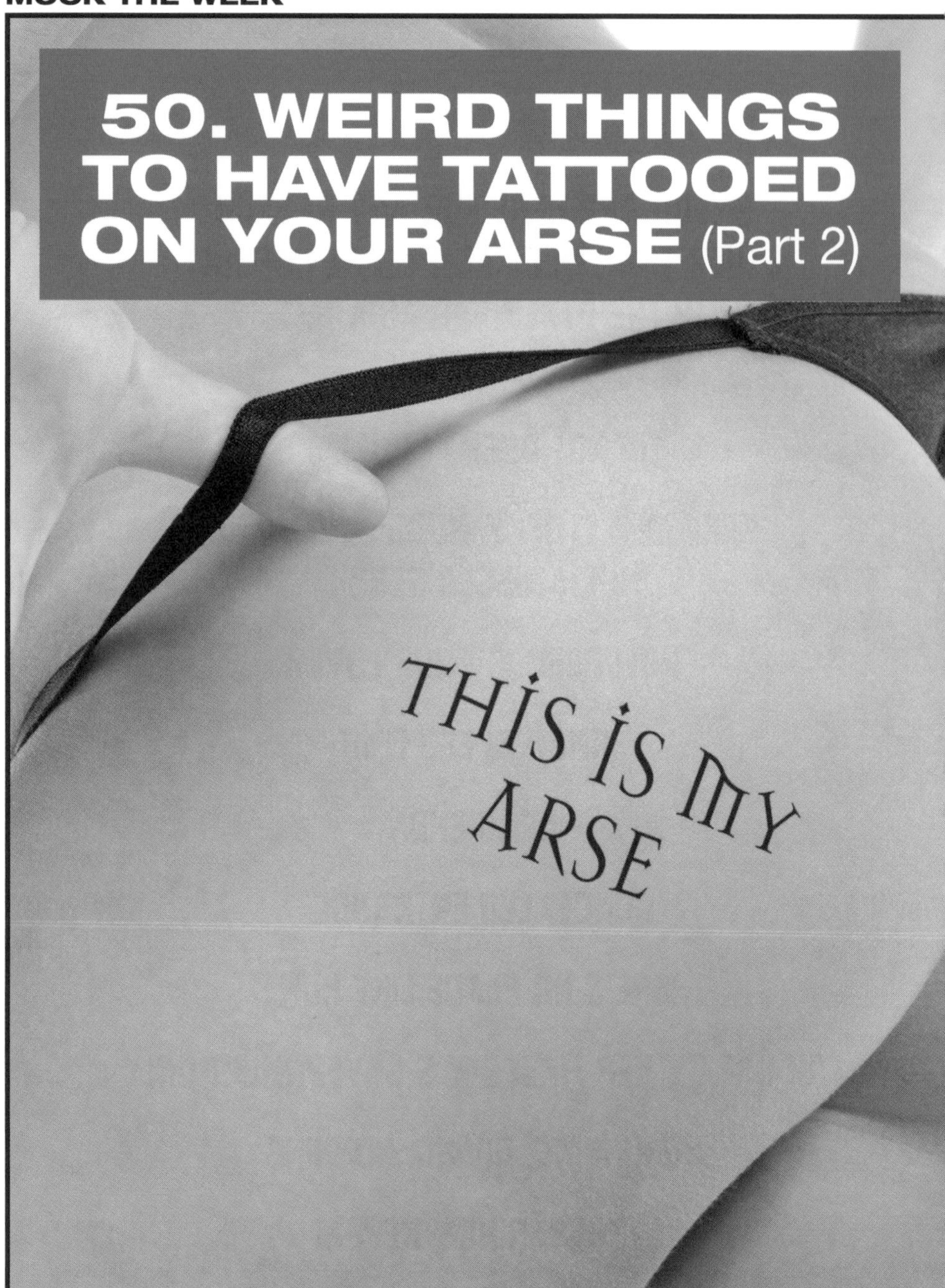

IF YOU ARE HERE FOR ANY REASON
OTHER THAN MEDICAL, PLEASE CONSULT
WITH THE OTHER END AS A MATTER
OF URGENCY

DO NOT OPEN IN PUBLIC

HERE LIES FLUFFY, MUCH LOVED AND
MUCH MISSED GERBIL

HOW DEEP IS YOUR LOVE?

30MPH SPEED LIMIT

DEAD END

CONCEALED ENTRANCE

THERE'S NO PLACE LIKE HOME

FOR USE BY HER MAJESTY'S GOVERNMENT ONLY

NO KISSING, DIVING, RUNNING

LATHER, RINSE, REPEAT

51. UNLIKELY COMPLAINTS TO THE BBC (Part 2)

Dear BBC, I am a huge fan of *Only Fools and Horses* and my friend told me of a hilarious bit where Del falls through a wine-bar counter. I've never seen it and don't believe it exists. Can you show it, please?

Dear BBC, I'm a middle-aged white male, degree educated. Where are *my* fucking programmes?

Dear BBC – everything on ITV, eh? It's shite.

As a music fan, I find it deeply frustrating that I have to sit through twenty-nine minutes of whining cockney misery before hearing a brief snatch of decent eighties synth drums.

Dear *Points of View*, is it true some of your letters are made up by us researchers here in the production office?

Dear BBC, can you warn us in advance if Andrew Lloyd Webber is about to appear on screen? A red triangle, perhaps?

Dear BBC, could you explain the plot of last week's *Murder, She Wrote*? It moved at too fast a pace for me.

Dear BBC, regarding *Can't Cook, Won't Cook* – they Can, and they Do.

Dear BBC, much as I enjoyed last night's *Nigella Express*, I must say the food somewhat detracted from her stupendous waps.

Dear BBC, I'm a little unhinged – if you read this letter out I'll kill myself.

Dear BBC, while watching *Road Runner* I was appalled at the continuing plugs for Acme products. Is this a legitimate use of licence payers' money?

Dear BBC, have you ever thought of bringing back *Doctor Who*?

Dear BBC, what's wrong with the British public? They just fill up the airwaves with their constant moaning. I can't stand it. I mean in my day, we just watched the TV and if we didn't like it we just had to put up with it. We were lucky to have one. I mean the kids today, don't get me started, with their mobile phones, their games consoles and their funny accents, I just don't understand them. Mind you, my wife doesn't understand *me*. I'd have an affair but I can't get an erection and I've got uncontrollable flatulence and halitosis. This is terrible at parties, not that we get invited out ever or if we do, not with anyone I'd actually want to spend any time with. Ooh, I've got a funny pain down my right arm, they're saying it's not a heart thing, but then what do you expect from the bloody NHS. They just don't want me to come in and use a bed. God forbid I should actually use something I pay my taxes for. I never go in there except when my old mum died on a trolley in A&E, misdiagnosis my arse. Two hours she was there in a puddle of her own piss, I mean I'm not one to moan, but . . .

52. UNLIKELY SIGNS (Part 1)

NO LAUGHING, SMILING OR WAVING

WORKMAN'S CLOTHES MUST BE WORN IN THIS GAY BAR

'KEEP BRITAIN OUT OF EUROPE' MEETING – 5 KILOMETRES

DANGER: SHARKS! JUST KIDDING. OR ARE WE?

IN CASE OF VANDALISM – BREAK GLASS

DO NOT FEED THE FERN BRITTON

CAUTION: TIME WARP AHEAD/BEHIND YOU

CAUTION: READING SIGNS ON MOTORWAY MAY CAUSE ACCIDENTS

AREA OF OUTSTANDING NATURAL BEAUTY OBSCURED BY SIGN

FOR LAND OF OZ – FOLLOW YELLOW BRICK ROAD

PLEASE DO NOT FEED THE ANIMALS, WE'RE TRYING TO STARVE THEM TO DEATH

No Parking-
Shitting
Pigeons
Above
DP
937

53. BAD THINGS TO HEAR AT CHRISTMAS

'So, we've all given each other goats in Ethiopia – how wonderful.'

'And remember, children, after every present you open, think of the bloodied corpse of the Lord Jesus nailed to a cross because of your sins.'

'My loyal subjects, Philip and I have had an eventful 2009; I got an intimate piercing and he is loving his Nintendo Wii shoot 'em up game.'

'And now on Channel 4, a Christmas special of *The Boy with No Head*.'

'Look – Granny's leaking from both ends.'

'So, that's a pet rabbit for Sally, and little Johnny gets an air rifle.'

'Daddy seems to have spent more on the au pair than me!'

'Me? I thought *you'd* turned the oven on.'

'There's a Constable Perkins at the door, dear, something about a missing barmaid.'

'Ah, another ill-conceived compilation CD. Thank you.'

'Hurrah! – there *is* a *My Family* Christmas special, after all.'

'Thank you, Vicar – a most enjoyable service. See you again next week.'

'Brilliant, a Dick and Dom Christmas special. That should bring the family together like Morecambe and Wise.'

'It's a long time since Uncle George went up to the toilet.'

'I'm sure Father Christmas put *Anal Babes* in your stocking by mistake.'

'So, I invited all these homeless people to share Christmas dinner with us, darling.'

'So, that's three who want to watch Chelsea v Man United, and four want to watch carols from King's College, Cambridge.'

'I'm sure Daddy would be delighted to help you build a scale model of HMS *Victory*, dear – I'll just wake him up.'

'Now, let's say a special prayer for Grandpa – who's doing time in Broadmoor.'

'Welcome to Hamleys, Sir. The toy you want is on the seventh floor.'

'Who's for figgy pudding? Surely we all want some figgy pudding?'

'What do you mean we should have taken the giblets out?'

'Sorry, love, I thought the shops would be open Christmas morning.'

'You promised Gran would be dead this Christmas.'

'Happy Winterval.'

'Good news, everyone, I've taped Noel Edmonds – to a chair in the cellar.'

'I've got you a hadron particle collider – and a million double-A batteries.'

'The man in the red suit who bounced you on his knee has been arrested.'

'Anyone want to go wassailing?'

54. ILL-ADVISED CHATROOM NAMES

Welcome Tony Lyons InSite-Login Apple .Mac Amazon eBay Yahoo! News (172) Apple (74)

Ill-advised chat rooms Search The Web UK Only Settings Sign In

Web Images Videos Q&A Beta More Showing 1-10 of 13,800,000

Alert: Filtering has occurred which reduced direct exposure to sexually explicit content.
I am over 18 and want to view all Adult Web results

Sponsored Results

Paedo In Disguise
Mushroom Arse
Scrotumface
Mahmoud Ahmadinejad
Valerie Singleton

Smalldick
I'm Really a Minger
Terrorist Mastermind
Racist
Rt Hon. Gordon Brown MP
Ignore Me
Harold Shipman's Ghost
Lembit Opik
Undercover Policeman
High on Meths
On the Verge of Suicide
Drug Dealer
Not Really 12, I'm 54
Assassinate Obama
W*nkf**ks**tc**t

55. UNLIKELY THINGS TO SEE IN A SCHOOL ATLAS

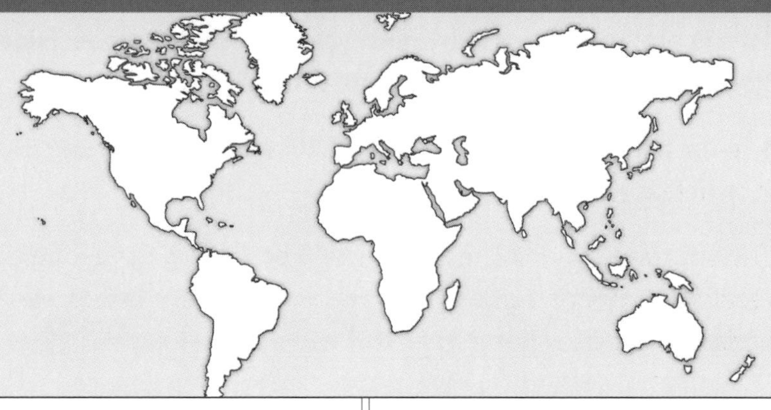

- The closer the contours are together, the more racist people are
- Here be dragons
- Bongo Bongo Land
- All the countries marked in green are where I've shagged a prozzie
- All branches of Subway are marked with an S
- Wops, Spics, Chinks, Paddies, Taffs, Jocks, Nips
- My Mum's
- The Lost City of Atlantis
- The Xs are where I hid the bodies
- Edge of the World where you'll fall off
- Green represents apple production and red, er, mass genocides
- Britain may look bigger than normal on this map, but that's because we're the best
- This colour represents vomit on the streets
- If Italy's the leg then Spain must be the snatch
- Atlas of the world in 300 million years' time: as you can see, it's pretty much all blue
- This atlas grades the women
- This is the world as it would have been if the beloved Führer had won
- This is Ceylon, or 'Sri Lanka', as we are supposed to bloody call it now
- El Salvador: the El stands for Leonard
- We have coloured these countries as to how much of a shithole they are
- That isn't a new island off Italy. My son had a cold

56. THINGS YOU WOULDN'T HEAR ON CHILDREN'S TV (Part 2)

'This is a picture sent in by nine-year-old Jane Davies. Nine? Bloody hell, I'd have said she was four. It's shit.'

'T is for twat, as in, "The producer, who is not renewing my contract, is a twat."'

'Frida is ready to hibernate and she'll be asleep for a long time, because someone not a million miles away from me drove their big flashy car over her in the BBC car park last night.'

'In this episode of *Hannah Montana* she discovers the fifteen-year-old boy she's been emailing is actually a forty-two-year-old lorry driver.'

'We're digging up the flower beds for the first time since 1987 to see ... ooh, what's this? Shit, it's a skull, arrggh!'

'"What's the matter?" said Pat to the lorry driver. "I've got loads of letters still to deliver."
"Try fucking indicating next time, you four-eyed twat."'

'And you take the fish like this and bite the head off, feel the warm blood ooze down your chin, mmm...'

'Every night, beneath the Arches of Waterloo Bridge, lies Andy Pandy, once one of the biggest stars on TV, now forgotten and fighting an increasingly hopeless battle with the bottle.'

'This is "snot".'

'That was the blue one, it's kind of smooth and mellow, this small purple one gives you more of a buzz.'

'Rupert, me Tiger Lily, me love you long time.'

'Tonight on *Science Quest*: is it safer to take it up the arse?'

'Edna the cow was crying. "Why so sad?" said Sammy the sheep. "Well, all my family are burning on that pyre over there." "You'll be next," said Sammy. "Here's the DEFRA man."'

'That was sent in by Iqbal Qasim. It wasn't really, one of our researchers drew it, but it makes us look more inclusive.'

'So with that one, I now have one in every single orifice. Join me next week on *Fun with Sprouts* to see how I got on.'

'This year's expedition was to Basra. John and I wanted to get stuck in, so we put on our body armour and set off. Unfortunately, John immediately stepped on a landmine, but we have got what's left of Shep.'

'What have we got in the sack? Let's have a look ... it's loads of hate mail and death threats for our Jewish presenter.'

'Next on *Blue Peter* – what to do with half a ton of elephant shit.'

57. UNLIKELY FRONT PAGE HEADLINES
Wednes
"Climate is fucking fucked" says Al Gore

CROSSRAIL TUNNEL UNCOVERS DOOR TO HELL

BROWN, BORIS & CAMERON SEX TAPE – AMAZING PICS

ELVIS FOUND READING LE NEWS ON FRENCH TV

BUSH CONVERTS TO ISLAM

BLUNKETT: I COULD SEE ALL ALONG

YOU WOULD, WOULDN'T YOU?

OI AFRICA! USE JOHNNIES! SAYS POPE

GOOGLE BOUGHT BY GINSTERS

SHARK BIT OFF MY HEAD AND I LIVED

MEN ARE LITERALLY FROM MARS, WOMEN ARE LITERALLY FROM VENUS SAYS DRAMATIC NEW STUDY

ALL PROBLEMS IN WORLD SOLVED

DRINK 16 BEERS A DAY SAY DOCTORS

NOT MUCH HAPPENING REALLY

OBAMA IN TOE STUB HORROR! 'OW' SCREAMS HOPPING PRESIDENT

FUCK YOU

IS THIS THE MYTHICAL LAND OF 'AUSTRALIA'? EXCLUSIVE PICTURES

OOH, MY LUNCH IS REPEATING ON ME A BIT

CHARLES CONSTRUCTS CHEESE VILLAGE IN CORNWALL

'YOU'RE ALL CTS,' SAYS QUEEN**

58. UNLIKELY PROPERTY MAGAZINE ADVERTS (Part 3)

• FOR SALE

Come and view it, you ct.**

Large Hackney townhouse would make ideal crack den.

Converted bungalow on airport flight path, may need renovation and possible extinguishing of still-smouldering jumbo jet.

Delightful Belfast terrace, comes with beautiful mural, metal shutters and is just a stone's throw from the lively local Catholic community.

Versatile property for sale conveniently located for shops – well, it's in the Tesco car park.

Fully furnished flat, quick sale due to owner's leprosy.

Home in grounds of Blenheim Palace, plans for skyscraper, roller disco and stock car racetrack awaiting permission.

Frankly miserable hovel would benefit from not viewing. Don't waste your time.

Gorgeous detached property with breathtaking view of the M6 flyover.

Immaculate mansion ruined by current owner's appalling taste. Worth viewing just for a laugh.

Large leather property for sale. Wall-to-wall fitted insoles. Room for many children. Old woman owner moving to larger footwear.

Grade I listed, completely unmodernized home dating back to 55 BC, original Roman features and in need of some excavation.

House for sale bears no resemblance to picture, otherwise you wouldn't even be reading this, believe me.

TO LET: room in 1970s house share. Repeated viewing. Apply R. Rigsby.

FOR SALE: American 1960s-style, family-run motel. Shower room in need of attention.

Unusual property for sale in Far East – large industrial complex in base of subterranean volcano. Would suit evil mastermind, or young couple.

Live like a king in this dream £15,000,000 residence. Something I'll never afford, yes, I'll be going home to my hovel in Leytonstone after showing some Russian gangster or sheikh round it. Bastards, life isn't fair. Well, I've had enough. Goodbye, cruel world ... arrrggh.

Home to one of the country's most famous names – feel free to come and have a nose round whether you want to buy it or not ... we're not supposed to tell you the owner, but the home will certainly give you some 'Satisfaction', he hasn't 'Painted it Black', but he does have some 'Brown Sugar' in the kitchen ...

59. LINES YOU WOULDN'T WANT TO HEAR IN A COSTUME DRAMA (Part 2)

'The Duchess is a lady of great moral rectitude, though I understand she goes like Stephenson's Rocket.'

'Take me, take me – in about thirty minutes, when I've got all these layers of clothing off ...'

'Your kind offer is both timely and indeed generous and should you, in all earnest, possess the wherewithal to vouchsafe its imminent presentation, I hazard to suggest it would be by no means unwelcome ... and could you put milk and two sugars in it?'

'You haven't paid for your papers, Mr Pickwick.'

'Yes, Darcy was haughty at the Meryton ball, but so what? He's loaded and hung like a donkey.'

'Tom Jones is late, but it's not unusual.'

'Lord Fauntwell has gone outside to take the air – and try to get a signal on his mobile.'

'This was the Old Curiosity Shop, but it's been bought by Subway.'

'Pls sir. I wd luv some more. Txt me back lol.'

'But, Miss Pendleton, this is a scene the Channel 4 commissioner insisted must be added – now get those bloomers off and join me in the lake.'

'Young Master Pip, you needn't visit upon me tonight, I'm going to stay in with my rampant rabbit.'

'That elderly spinster from the village – wasn't she M from the James Bond films?'

'Why, Mr Knightley, you've got me smelling like a fishmonger's slab.'

'You have arrived here on your trusty steed, but half an hour late. So that's a guinea off my pizza.'

'You say the Brothers Karamazov have all gone to England to buy football clubs?'

'Do you like my new carriage? You'll be seeing a lot of it because we spent half the budget on it.'

'My lords and ladies: Colonel and Mrs Celebrity Walk-on. The Duke of American Co-Star for Overseas Sales. The Reverend Comedy Star Who Can't Really Act ... and Dame Judi Dench. Again.'

'I've journeyed two and a half days to get here from York. There was a contraflow on the M1.'

60. UNLIKELY AIRCRAFT SAFETY ANNOUNCEMENTS

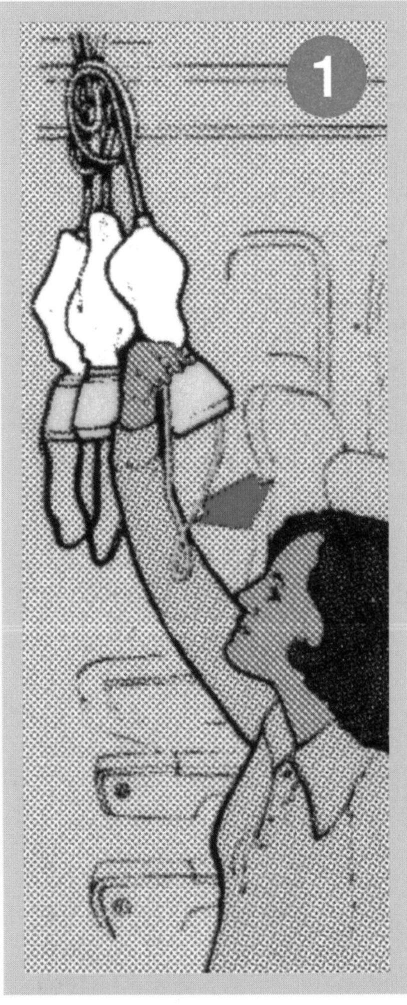

'Please fit your own oxygen mask before taking pleasure in the fruitless fight for breath of others.'

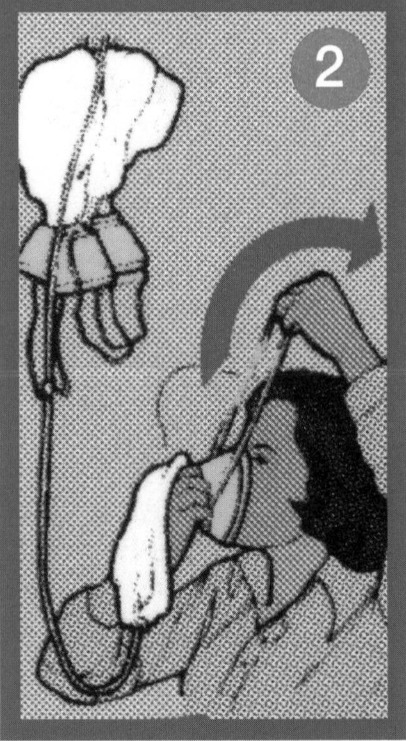

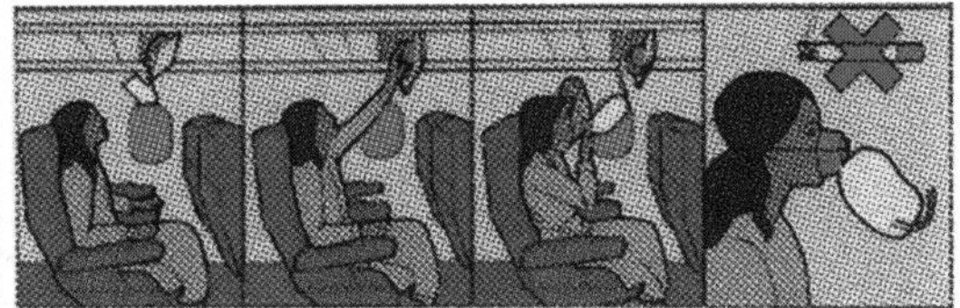

'Keep your seatbelt fastened at all times, though if we do crash, its only function will be to keep your body stationary as it burns.'

'The cabin floor is fitted with lights in case of smoke or the arrival of Siegfried and Roy.'

'Your safety is our number one priority, obviously apart from our operating profit, which is secured by buying old reconditioned planes and cutting back on mechanical checks.'

'If you know how to fly and land a plane, it is always useful to make yourself known to a flight attendant before take off, just in case.'

'In the event of a serious incident, prayer sheets are found in your seat pocket and our in-flight crew are happy to dispense final sexual acts in the toilets to the front, middle and rear.'

'We'll now show you the procedure for a landing on water, but you don't have to bother watching this bit, because if we have to ditch in the Pacific you'll either die instantly or the sharks will get you.'

'The lifejacket is located under your seat, next to the stinking feet of the man behind you.'

'The toilet is fitted with a smoke detector and also a hidden camera, for the enjoyment of Bernd, our chief air steward.'

'This is how you undo your seatbelt, although let's be honest, if you can't do this then you really shouldn't be on this plane in the first place.'

61. LINES YOU NEVER HEAR IN THE SOAPS

'Oi, Peggy, I can't drink this, your bra has just twanged off and landed in my pint.'

'Harold, guess what: the government have decided to hand Ramsay Street back to the Aborigines.'

'Ricky, get in here quick, we're on telly, having this conversation.'

'Dot, if you sold your house in Albert Square, you'd be able to buy a nice place in the country.'

'You know, for a small street in a quiet suburb of Manchester, there's an incredible turnover of people.'

'I'm fed up of the Queen Vic, let's go somewhere else.'

'I'm sorry, you're too old, fat and dark-haired to live in Hollyoaks.'

'Isn't it incredible that whenever you open the door to go out in Ramsay Street, someone is always standing there?'

'You've really changed. Not just your personality, but also the way you look and speak.'

'I had a car crash because we needed to use the Erinsborough Hospital set again.'

'I'm really annoyed with you. Let's go over to the Queen Vic and have a huge row in front of everyone.'

'So, that's resolved everything and everyone's fine.' (B-Dum Dum dum dum dum)

'Bad news about the band we've booked for the wedding. Only the drummer's turned up.' (B-Dum Dum dum dum dum)

'Oh, no! The synth drum's broken!' (B-Dum–)

'Oh, Phil, I'm so proud of you, becoming Walford's first BNP councillor.'

'We don't need to talk.'

'Hey, guys, are we in *Neighbours* or *Home and Away*?'

'What we need is some sort of transparent gimmick to make this end on a spurious moment of suspense.'

'This is the fucking East End, I'll fucking swear if I fucking want to.'

'Blimey, doesn't anyone in Albert Square own a washing machine?'

'Poor old Dot, she seems to be going through some pseudo-psychological existential crisis ...'

'The Queen Vic's changed management. It's now a gay pub.'

'Phil, I'm leaving the Arches, I've finally got funding for my PhD.'

62. THINGS YOU DON'T WANT TO HEAR ON A SEX PHONE LINE

'I'm eating a bacon and egg sandwich and the brown sauce is going all over me flip-flops.'

'Yer big poof.'

'I'm hung like a fieldmouse.'

'Ooh, yes, that feels good ... sorry, I'm at the chiropractor's.'

'OK, I'm putting on my jumper.'

'I'm standing at Clapham Junction and I can see the B4765 pulling in to Platform 12.'

'Hello, this sex call has been outsourced to Bangalore. Can I be helping you to come, Sir?'

'118118, would you like to be put straight through if you know what I mean, Madam?'

'This is John Prescott, and since I retired I've been contemplating the exploration of sexual fantasticat ... oh, bollocks, pass us me mini kievs...'

'I'm wearing a negligee and I'm rubbing ... what do you mean you're on *Who Wants to Be a Millionaire?*'

'I'm Melody, I'm short and fat and I've lost most of my teeth.'

'You're being a very naughty boy ... so I'm hanging up.'

'I'm Danielle, or Daniel – your choice.'

'Your call is very important to us, please continue to hold.'

'Press 1 for Northern, 2 for Brummie, 3 for an Essex slapper, otherwise please hold and take pot luck on whichever of our low-rent, unattractive prostitutes becomes available first.'

'What am I doing? I'm cutting my toenails.'

63. UNLIKELY SIGNS (Part 2)

NO RUNNING, NO JUMPING, NO FUCKING UP THE ARSE

STAND CLEAR OF THE DOORS – THE LOCK'S A BIT DODGY, THEY COULD OPEN AT ANY TIME

BY ORDER OF HM GOVT, IF YOU'RE HAPPY AND YOU KNOW IT, YOU MUST CLAP YOUR HANDS

PLEASE DO NOT KISS THE ANIMALS

YOU DON'T HAVE TO BE MAD TO WORK HERE – BECAUSE THAT WOULD BE AN IRRESPONSIBLE EMPLOYMENT PRACTICE

GOLF SALE SIGN SALE, 200 YARDS

CAUTION: GUARD DOGS. AND ONCE THEY CATCH YOU, THEY'LL WANT TO PLAY FETCH FOR HOURS

UNATTENDED LUGGAGE WILL BE TAKEN AWAY, RIFLED THROUGH AND THEN PUT BACK

STAND WELL BACK FROM THE PLATFORM EDGE, IF YOU'RE TRYING TO COMMIT SUICIDE, A RUN UP'S ALWAYS BEST

BRITAIN WELCOMES CHEAP HARD-WORKING POLES

Caution-
Misleading
Sign

64. BAD *QUESTION TIME* QUESTIONS (Part 2)

'I'd like to ask the minister what it's like to be shat on by a rent boy.'

'With respect, Harriet Harman, you're evading the question. Just what colour panties are you wearing?'

'I disagree with David Miliband's answer. Would he like to come outside and discuss it further in the car park?'

'I've just popped in from the *Weakest Link* studio next door, can any of the panel tell me what "B" is a country in South America: Brazil or Argentina?'

'Are you related to Richard Dimbleby?'

'Can I just ask David Cameron what measures he would take as Prime Minister to wipe that smug grin off his face?'

'The usual panel this week: a Labour MP, a Tory MP, a Lib Dem you've never heard of, a hard-faced businesswoman and David Baddiel.'

'Has everyone on the panel got their brown wings?'

'I'd like to ask Alistair Darling a question, but only so I can say "Darling" in the question and get a cheap laugh.'

'Next clichéd whinge, please.'

'I'd like to ask Hazel Blears … where are you? STAND UP!'

'I'd like to ask Geoff Hoon if he knows where the bogs are, please?'

'Can I have a round of applause, please?'

'Does anyone on the panel have a cock as big as this?'

'Samantha Cameron, you would, wouldn't you?'

'Are you trying to seduce me, Mr Dimbleby?'

'If we are a cross-section of society, does that really mean that the country is full of ugly, ill-informed people?'

'This is a question for Kerry Katona …'

65. UNLIKELY SMALL ADS (Part 2)

FOR SALE

Amuse your friends – tell them you paid £20 for this load of shit.

Write underwater with this bath. Pen not included.

FOR SALE: pack of polos. Mint condition.

Formula One boss seeks Ein Deutsche Mädchen für grossen buttockslappen. Phone this number and ask for Granddad.

One aspirin for sale, 5p or nearest offer.

Be my mate and I'll spend millions on you every day. Robert Mugabe.

Bespectacled middle-aged *Star Trek* enthusiast seeks non-inflatable woman.

FOR SALE: one canoe, hardly used. Also – flat in Panama – genuine reason for sale – apply Durham Prison and ask for Stupid.

Recent divorcee WLTM rich sugar daddy to lavish gifts on me. I am blonde and leggy (one).

Real X-ray specs, apply Radiology Unit, Harefield Hospital. £500,000 ONO. (Not really specs, more of a room with a big machine in it. You didn't get it from me.)

Giant pyramid for sale in Giza, buyer collects.

Series of golden arches collected over last decade. Not stolen from McDonalds at all, however it might look. £5 for the lot.

Box of 'Giuliani for President' T-shirts, $3 each or, oh sod it, just have them.

Bubbly fifty-something seeks man who likes fat grandmothers.

Soiled underwear from maximum-security mental institution, make me an offer.

Illegal pirate videos for sale, good quality apart from when that bloke in front gets up to go to the toilet in *Cloverfield*.

Canderel dispenser for sale, does not include Canderel.

Two cheeky, lovable Geordie TV stars, GSOH, why not phone us, calls will cost no more than £1 a minute.

Trunk full of Diana, Princess of Wales's belongings. Make me an offer. P Burrell (not that one).

Original Van Gogh for sale £50 million ONO. Frame not included. Would make ideal present for someone who knows nothing about art and doesn't watch *Crimewatch*. Slight rip in top corner.

Fresh manure for sale, loads of the stuff, £10 per bucket, buyer collects. P.S. Also plumber needed urgently.

Beautiful wife for sale, 40, blonde, curvaceous, would suit necrophiliac. Buyer collects.

66. BAD THINGS TO SAY ON A FIRST DATE (Part 1)

'You remind me of my eighth wife.'

'No alcohol for me – I'm trying to get pregnant.'

'I'm stuffed – I can't eat another thing. Not if you're expecting anal.'

'No one knows where you are, do they?'

'No food for me, thanks, I'll just have wine.'

'I'll have a dump before eating. I don't need to move, I'm wearing a nappy.'

'Flowers for a lovely lady – I took a shortcut via the graveyard.'

'I'm a bit of a regular here – I can thoroughly recommend the Happy Meal.'

'If you didn't want me looking down your top you shouldn't have worn one so low-cut. Anyway, I'd better get back to my date now.'

'I've been told it's cleared up so I can't wait to try it out.'

'I thought it best if we met in a disused warehouse.'

'Would you like to come back to my place and see my life-size matchstick model of Barry George?'

'Please don't ask me if that dress makes you look fat.'

'I never wear underwear – it aggravates my genital rash.'

'You are so sexy, will you excuse me while I go to the bathroom and masturbate?'

'Would you like to come back to my place for a quick nightcock, sorry, cap?'

'I think it's sweet that you're a vegetarian. I'll have the sheep's brains and tripe, please.'

'I'm not like other men – I'm a violent rapist.'

'I didn't have any rice so I'm not paying for that.'

'I'd suggest dinner, but I'm not allowed cutlery.'

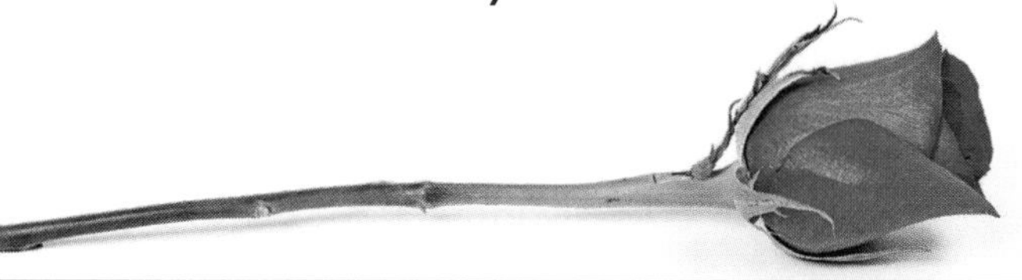

67. REJECTED EXAM QUESTIONS (Part 2)

1. Describe the reproductive system of the frog without getting an erection.
2. Jane Austen was an anteater. She was. How do you know? Were you there? No. So there. Discuss.
3. Out a gay member of staff at your school using hearsay, maliciousness and homophobia.
4. It is red and itches a bit, but has stopped throbbing since Thursday. What the fuck is wrong with me? For extra marks: should I see a doctor?
5. Baljit and Susan are working together to help Wang dig a hole. Express as a percentage how politically correct this question is.
6. How easy are GCSEs, man?
7. Why do fools fall in love? Give examples with references to birds singing gay.
8. If Mary had £1 million in savings in 1976 and invested half at a rate of 5 per cent and the other half at a rate of 7 per cent in 1992, but lost it all last year, calculate her total losses and why the fuck I married her.
9. Which do you prefer: jazz, or jam? Please show your workings.
10. Complete this sequence: 1, 2, 3, 4, 5, 6, 7, 8 …
11. Compare the methods of characterization and plot development in *The Da Vinci Code* with *The Highway Code*.
12. Using only the English language, please write something.

13. Please give examples.

14. If Gladys had 10 pillowcases, John had 8 pillowcases and Robert … oh, fuck this. I wanted to be a novelist when I was your age. How did it come to this? Take my advice. Get up now, sod the exam and go and enjoy yourself. They're all a waste of time.

15. What has been the greater weapon in political dialogue in the last few years: bathos, rhetoric or blackmail?

16. Humpty Dumpty sat on the wall. Humpty Dumpty had a great …?

17. Which of these options should you do if you are happy and you know it?

18. Write your name here. Please show your workings.

19. Name a business like showbusiness.

20. Complete this sequence by writing in your PIN number.

21. Give the person behind you oral sex using tongue, teeth and saliva.

22. Are you going to vote Labour when you're older? We'll give you an A*.

23. Discuss Shakespeare's use of nocturnal imagery in *The Tempest* with reference to the stuff you wrote on your arm last night when revising.

24. Is it me or is it stuffy in here? Discuss.

25. 4, 4, 4, 3, 1, 2, 1, 2, 1. What is the next number in this sequence of Arsenal's league position under Arsène Wenger?

26. Do you suffer from memory loss? Call this number for a free month's trial of our kit.

68. THINGS YOU WON'T HEAR ON BREAKFAST TV

'WAKEY WAKEY! Come on, get up, you're going to miss your bus. Come on, don't make me come up there! This is what happens when you go to bed as late as that. Get up, you lazy bastard!'

'Morning, Britain. Bloody hell, you look like I feel.'

'And now your chance to win £10,000 with Keith Chegwin – will he stick his cock through your letterbox?'

'I'm not saying I'm tired, but the bags under my eyes look like scrotums.'

'And now, over from America, a guest I give a fuck about.'

'I'll now interview another nutter with a mad theory for the next ten minutes. Not because he's any good, but we can never get people in this early.'

'It's six o'clock, I haven't had time for a shower and my tights are stuck to me.'

'Here's some footage of my stomach band being fitted.'

'I get up at 2 a.m. every day, I'm on the edge. Yesterday I killed a man.'

'Now the news, where Penny Smith will try and be funny.'

'Hey, call in sick, there's some great stuff on later, porn and everything.'

'Morning, Britain, I had a cracking vindaloo last night, good job it isn't smellovision.'

'If you've just woken up with an erection, here's Suzy with the weather.'

'I haven't been to bed!!!'

'It takes me more time to look like this than it took John Hurt to get made up for *The Elephant Man*.'

'I get up at 3 a.m. every day for this job and I wonder why my wife's fucking the postman.'

'And now, Lorraine Kelly will attempt to conduct an interview without telling her guest they "look gorgeous" or using the word "boobies".'

'So now let's have a look at the new "haemorrhoid cam".'

GOOD MORNING

69. BAD THINGS TO SAY AT A WEDDING (Part 2)

'If the bride would raise her veil, I will invite the groom to kiss the ... whoa, Jesus, rather you than me, son.'

'Now a photo of the bridesmaids ... lovely ... if you can just lose your tops.'

'Paul has met a beautiful woman, someone he gets on with, who shares his interests and loves him as much as he loves her, but he realized last night that he had to forget about her and get on with the business of marrying Sandra.'

'Wow. You *are* wearing white. I thought it was a joke.'

'I've known the groom for twelve years. We met in a club in London and had a passionate one-night stand before deciding we worked better as friends.'

'Rashid is delighted to be marrying Linda and getting a British passport... but obviously more the marrying Linda bit.'

'I'm here to talk to you about international loan financing.'

'May I offer a roast to the bridesmaids. Sorry, toast!'

'If anyone here knows of any just cause or impediment ... bloody hell, form a queue, let's do this one at a time.'

'Please don't throw confetti – or bottles.'

'Can I just say how lovely the mother of the bride looks ... when she's about to come.'

'They are a well-matched couple with great intelligence – believe me, I just ran my eyes over the pre-nup, and it's watertight.'

HILARY & KEITH:
LOVE, DESTINY &
UNEXPECTED PREGNANCY

70. UNLIKELY THINGS TO READ IN A SCHOOL FRENCH BOOK

CHAPTER 10

1. If Mademoiselle Fifi can entertain three gentlemen an hour, how much can she make in a day?

2. Everyday French Situations, Exercise 4: Signing for Arsenal.

3. Et maintenant, l'histoire de le battle de Agincourt.

4. Write an essay on President Sarkozy without mentioning his wife's baps.

5. Here are Monsieur Vernier, Madame Vernier, and Granddad Vernier, who collaborated during the war.

6. Remember – if during your French exam you don't know an answer, just shrug your shoulders and go, 'Pffff.'

7. Chapters 18–39: *The Rules of Boules*.

8. If you must set fire to British lamb, please wait until the lorry is out of the Channel Tunnel.

9. Write a letter to your French pen pal, Hélène, telling her about yourself, where you live and encouraging her to send back photographs of herself in her underwear.

CHAPTER 10: J'AIME LE FROMAGE

10. Napoleon was a silly little twat. Discuss.

11. There is no French word for Ladyshave, deodorant or fighting till the last man.

12. Once you have learned French, you will be able to read Proust, Jean-Paul Sartre, and listen to French opera in the original language. But it's not all bad news.

13. Translate the following sentence: 'Why bother to learn French? They all speak English anyway.'

14. True or false? France has given the world great pop music.

15. Useful French phrases:

'What cheese is this?'
'This is nice cheese.'
'Where is the cheese?'
'Can I have some more cheese?'
'I admire this cheese, I like a strong cheese.'
'Do you mind if I just hold your cheese?'
'At home I have five different cheeses.'
'Can I see the cheese board please?'
'You have a lovely selection of cheese.'
'Hey you, get off of my cheese.'
'President de Gaulle was a great Frenchman and he liked cheese a lot.'
'Have you only got fucking cheese?'

71. UNLIKELY SIGNS (Part 3)

CAUTION CROSSING CHILDREN – THEY'VE PROBABLY GOT KNIVES, KEEP YOUR DOORS LOCKED

IF YOU CAN READ THIS YOU'RE GAY

PLEASE DO NOT SHIT ON THE SEATS

WATCH OUT ... TOO LATE

NO SIGNS FOR 50 MILES

IN CASE OF EMERGENCY – INFORM SUPERMAN

WARNING: FALLING STOCKBROKERS

DANCE CLASS AHEAD – SLOW, SLOW, QUICK QUICK SLOW

PLEASE DO NOT TAKE THE OPPORTUNITY TO ENJOY YOURSELF IN THIS POOL

PLEASE IGNORE THIS SIGN

WHEN BLACK FLAG IS VISIBLE, GO IN THE SEA IF YOU MUST, BUT DON'T SAY WE DIDN'T WARN YOU

WARNING: YOU ARE BEING SURVEYED BY CAMERA, THIS WILL CONTINUE FOR 24 HOURS, EVEN WHEN YOU LEAVE HERE AND GO HOME

WARNING!
CHEESE

72. UNLIKELY LINES FROM FAIRY TALES

And Cinderella and the prince lived happily ever after, until their carriage crashed in a Parisian road tunnel.

'Keep rubbing,' said the genie, 'and something magical will come out, if you know what I mean.'

'Old Mother Hubbard, we're from the NSPCC and we're acting on a tip-off.'

'Look, I know the duckling's different, but that's no excuse for calling him names. He's not ugly, he's just alternatively plumed.'

'Look, Snow White, it's great having you around, but this was only meant to be temporary so me and the lads think if you're going to stay you might have to start stumping up for the council tax.'

'Actually, Rapunzel, since you've had your Brazilian, there's much less for me to climb up.'

'Mr Bear, sorry to bother you, but we've had reports of an intruder in the area. You haven't noticed any porridge being taken have you?'

Tom, Tom, the piper's son, stole a pig and was beheaded live on Al Jazeera.

'Red Riding Hood, you are not going out dressed like that, you look like you're gagging for it.'

'There's been a terrible accident – is there a doctor with vinegar and brown paper?'

And Baby Bear said, 'Look who's sleeping in my bed – spread 'em, Blondie.'

The third pig made his house out of bricks – which soon plummeted in value.

Tom, Tom, the piper's son – invented satnav.

Unfortunately, it was bad luck for Prince Charming, as when he woke up Camilla had turned back into an old boot.

'Meet my fellow dwarfs, Snow White: Anal, Oral, Doggy, Jizzy, Fisty and Bashful.'

Half a pound of tupenny rice – costs a billion dollars in Zimbabwe.

Humpty Dumpty had a great fall – remember, egg-based characters can go down as well as up.

73. BAD NAMES FOR RESTAURANTS

Sam & Ella's

Norovirus

Leftovers

Offal World

Sprout-u-like

Yo Doggy!

Cannibals

Beef Curtains

It'll Do

Battery-Farmed Fried Chicken

Mad Cows

Retchers

Crippen's Chop House

Litvinenko's

Cannibal Hut

PISS HUT
PIZZA
OPEN
NO SMOKING

74. REJECTED EXAM QUESTIONS (Part 3)

1. Was your reaction to the previous question a) 'Yeesss!', b) 'Hmmm', or c) 'Shiiittt!'?
2. Use the pen and paper provided to do some maths and stuff.
3. If Chris robs Peter to pay Paul, why did he get involved in this process in the first place?
4. Show us your tits for an automatic A*.
5. You're shit, and you know you are. Discuss.
6. Peter is older than John and John is older than Mary, but they are all far too young to be doing what I'm paying them for. How long am I going to get?
7. Think of a number, double it, take two, add three, divide by two, multiply by five, add three, take away six. Have you got the number you first thought of? You haven't? Bollocks, it normally works.
8. How many words do you have to change from an answer downloaded off the Internet to not be accused of cheating?
9. Parlez-vous français? Answer: a) oui, b) 31, c) an elephant.
10. Why is it that when your exam results come out, the papers only print pictures of pretty girls?
11. John has a knife, Peter has a gun but no knife, Andy has a knife, a gun and an axe. Which gangs are they in?
12. Using the mirror provided, copy the answer off that lad next to you.

13. Rewrite *War and Peace* using words of one syllable but making it better than Tolstoy's original.

14. Shakespeare is shit and that innit. Discuss.

15. If John, who is 5 ft 11 in. tall, bumps into Paul – who is 5 ft 7 in.– in the pub, calculate the angle Paul would need to raise a 7 in. pint glass to stab John in the face.

16. In no more than 1,000 words write out 'Pointless' 1,000 times.

17. If my dad is bigger than your dad, what the fuck are you going to do about it?

18. If Michael spent £800,000 on a house 18 months ago and that house has decreased 37 per cent in value, calculate how long Michael will be able to resist alcoholism and suicide.

19. Mark has lost a leg but grown an arm. Peter has lost a head and grown two legs. Which one will be the subject of a Channel 4 documentary first?

20. Chemistry – what percentage of Jordan is silicon?

21. If your midfielder is worth £20 million, how much do you inflate the price when Man City enquire about him?

22. Insert the following up your anus and chart the results on a bar graph.

23. What is the 654th word of the sixth Harry Potter book?

24. Jeremy Kyle – why?

25. Haven't you finished yet, you moron?

75. BAD THINGS TO SAY AT A STATE BANQUET

'Stand up if you hate the French.'

'What the fuck is this?'

'Yeah? Well I'm Emperor of the Universe.'

'What do you mean, "Stop slurping?"'

'Pull my finger.'

'I'll just have a lager top please, chief.'

'Argggh, a dog, kill it, kill it!'

'You're that rich bastard who shot my osprey.'

'Quick, Diana, get back in your cupboard! The guests haven't gone yet.'

'Which twat got the last spud?'

'Three German officers crossed the Rhine, parlez-vous...'

'You're the French ambassador? Yeah, right.'

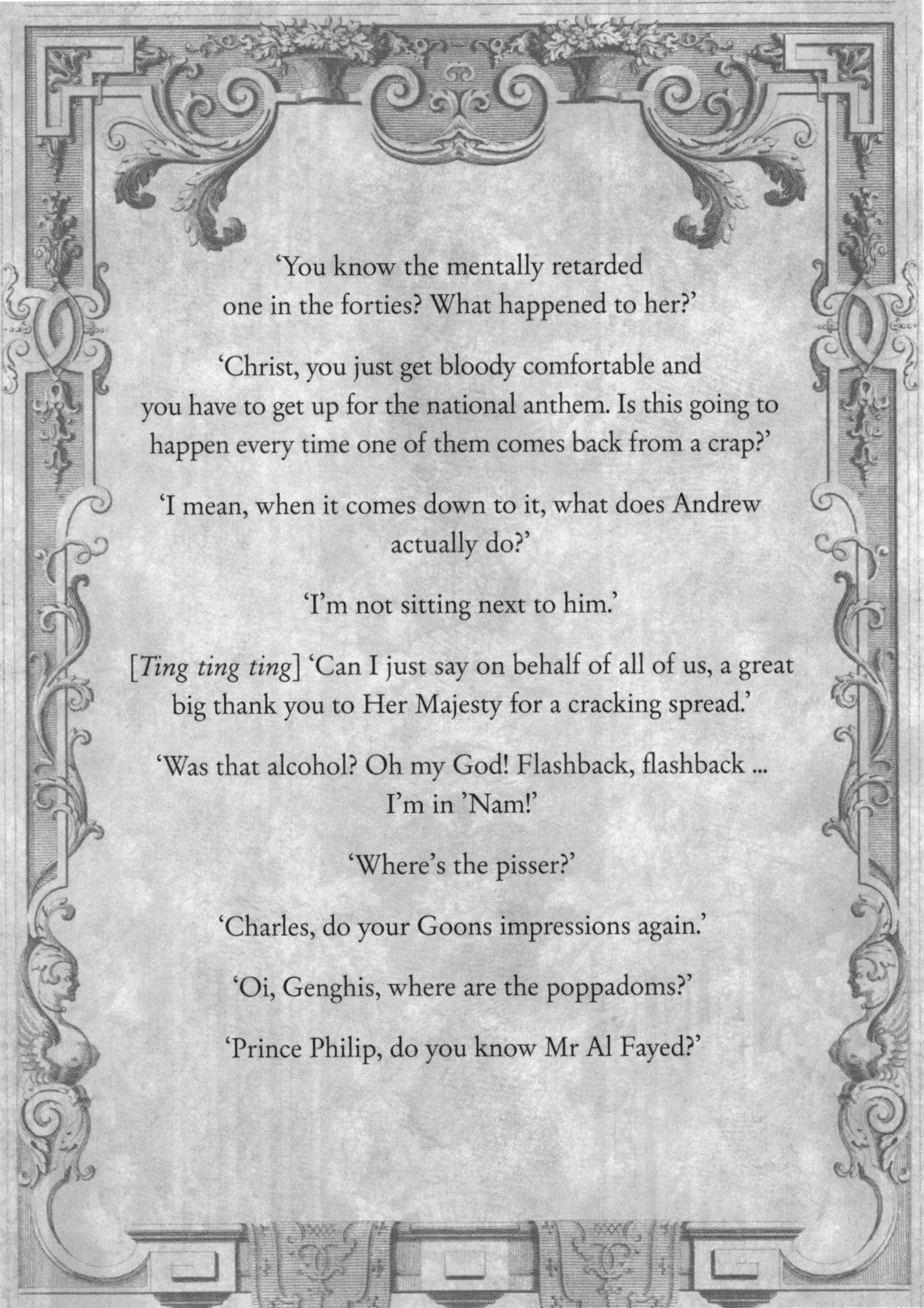

'You know the mentally retarded one in the forties? What happened to her?'

'Christ, you just get bloody comfortable and you have to get up for the national anthem. Is this going to happen every time one of them comes back from a crap?'

'I mean, when it comes down to it, what does Andrew actually do?'

'I'm not sitting next to him.'

[*Ting ting ting*] 'Can I just say on behalf of all of us, a great big thank you to Her Majesty for a cracking spread.'

'Was that alcohol? Oh my God! Flashback, flashback ... I'm in 'Nam!'

'Where's the pisser?'

'Charles, do your Goons impressions again.'

'Oi, Genghis, where are the poppadoms?'

'Prince Philip, do you know Mr Al Fayed?'

76. UNLIKELY THINGS TO READ IN A RECIPE BOOK

Squeeze cheese out of tube and on to cracker. Spread.

Completed meal will bear no resemblance to picture.

Take one raw, still-beating pig's heart.

If you can't get Sevruga caviar, fish paste will do just as well.

Remove penis, wipe on curtains. Light cigarette, go to sleep.

After three hours, open the oven, realize you're two hours too late, and phone for a pizza.

For a less fattening version of this dessert, don't eat so much of it.

Then add the eye of toad, and leg of newt, and leave to hubble and bubble for 15 minutes.

I love to scoop up the last traces of this naughty sauce straight from the bowl, and then lick my fingers suggestively, while I'm being fucked across the kitchen table.

Smooth the icing, now remove your pants and sit on it till done.

Take the chicken kievs out of the freezer, then peer at them closely, and guess whether the sell-by date says 09 or 00.

And, hey presto, a perfect lemon jizz cake!

Take your very sharpest sushi knife and very carefully creep up behind your cheating bastard of a husband.

Mince, pour, serve – is all you need to do as a cocktail waiter.

Serves four, or one really greedy c**t.

Add salt, vinegar, ketchup and eat.

Serves one lonely alcoholic bastard.

Boil kettle, pour on, wait fifteen seconds, serve.

Ingredients: two bottles of vodka, ice, tonic water. On second thoughts, sod the tonic water, and actually the ice is optional as well.

Take a knob of butter (so that's between 1 and 14 inches, depending on how much of a man you are).

Drain the blood, remove clothes, jewellery, dice and serve.

Delia's recipe: add alcohol, wait forty-five minutes, take one microphone and then walk onto pitch at Carrow Road.

Leave for thirty minutes, then add petrol.

Pour contents in, leave out and await botulism.

This will take at least nine hours to prepare. You might be better buying the same thing in Tesco.

Add the panda and hey presto!

Mix carefully, holding nose and trying not to gag.

A variation on his 'n' hers desserts – one for fat people and one for the normal.

Knead until hard, then ejaculate.

Do not operate heavy machinery with this meal.

Add cream, chocolate, stir, eat, vomit in toilets.

When baked hard, remove from oven and throw at husband.

Stir and stand on windowsill for an hour. No, not you, the fucking cake, dickhead!

If at this point it has not risen, cancel dinner party.

Place both breasts onto worktop in order to distract dinner guests from the shit food.

Remove socks and wade around in it for a bit.

Leave to stand for at least six hours or so, then tape behind radiator, sell house, move, thus making it uninhabitable for the new owners.

Make sure you wash your hands thoroughly, especially if you've just had a really steamy, runny shit.

And if you can't find an apple to put in the pig's mouth, a budgerigar or hamster will suffice.

Ingredients: blood, semen and cheese of your choice.

Best served between salad and dessert course when conversation has taken a racist turn.

77. MODERN NURSERY RHYMES

Little Boy Blue, come bring your bolt gun, the sheep are all waiting, the cows have been done.

The Grand old Duke of York, he had 10,000 men,
and his regiment was merged with the
King's Own Humpty Together-Putters.

Bobby Davro's all at sea,
He's not seen on ITV,
He'll turn up on QVC,
Poor old Bobby Davro.

Georgie Porgie pudding and pie,
invaded Iraq but didn't know why.

Who killed Cock Robin? Who saw him die?
Was it you? The police have set up an incident room and there is a substantial reward.

Jack be nimble, Jack be quick, but there are health and safety issues re: the whole candlestick-jumping thing.

Hickory Dickory Dock,
A mouse ran up my cock,
You can see it on YouTube.

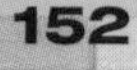

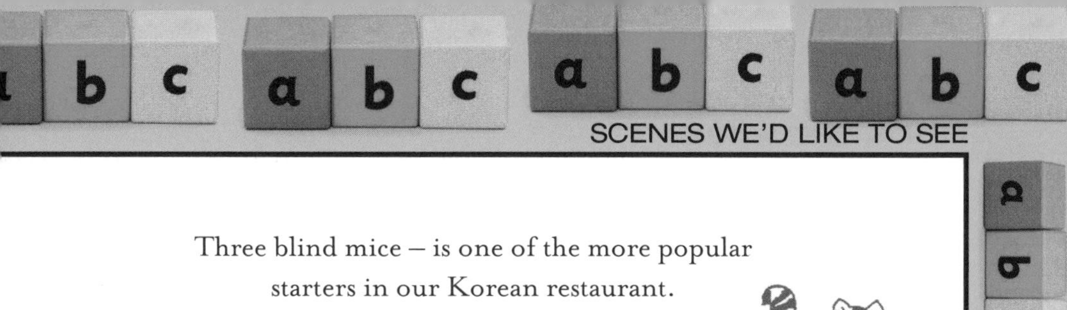

Three blind mice – is one of the more popular
starters in our Korean restaurant.

Here we go round the mulberry bush,
The mulberry bush, mulberry bush,
Here we go round the mulberry bush,
I hate this bloody satnav.

Hey diddle diddle,
MPs on the fiddle,
The tabloids are over the moon.

There was an old lady who swallowed a fly –
she waited in casualty for ten hours and died.

Old King Cole was a merry old soul until he
was ousted in a brutal military coup.

Lavender's blue, dilly dilly,
Lavender's green,
The plasma screen's on the blink again.

Jack and Jill went up the hill,
To have underage sex.

Jack Sprat would eat no fat,
It had just been siphoned out of Fern Britton.

Little Boy Blue,
Come blow your horn,
I'll download the image,
in a file called Porn.

78. BAD THINGS TO SAY ON A FIRST DATE (Part 2)

'Let's share the peas. One for you, one for me, one for you, one for me ...'

'Before I offer to pay the bill, can I just check that we are going to have sex later?'

'How many children do you want?'

'You don't drink? Oh, fucking hell!!'

'My favourite colour? Spurting-blood red, I think.'

'I like big women – why are you crying?'

'Let's have lunch here, then go on to the *Doctor Who* convention.'

'We can go back to my place, my wife's a heavy sleeper.'

'To mark our first date I'd like to return the underwear I stole off your washing line.'

'The tie? Why, it's made from the skin of my former victims.'

'I'll order a bottle of the house red, and would you like anything to drink?'

'Sorry about that, I've followed through. I hope you're upwind.'

'Wow! Let me just look at you in that low-cut top. HONK HONK.'

'Yes, it is a gun in my pocket.'

'Just wait while I switch my camera on.'

'I hope you like dogs – I'm serving one with rice and salad.'

'I'd like to sit down, but as you'll find out, I've got a prolapsed anus.'

'You're strong, aren't you? The drugs should have started to work by now.'

'My favourite film director? I don't know – who made *Shaven Vixens VI*?'

'Shall we go Dutch? You can come back to my place and sit naked in the window.'

79. UNLIKELY TV LISTINGS

TV LISTINGS

Wednesday 21st

9.00 a.m. **Make Me an Egghead**
Dermot Murnaghan performs brainwashing and plastic surgery on members of the public to make them terminally dull.

9.30 a.m. **Cops, Cops, Cops**
Fantastically cheap-to-make programme where policemen and women put on an act for the cameras and let black people go with a cheery word of warning.

11.00 a.m. **The C**nty W**ky Tits show**
Cutting-edge comedy on Channel 4 hosted by Mark Dolan and an 8 ft rubber vagina.

12.00 p.m. **Egyptian Nazi Sharks II**
Channel 5's popular documentary series returns.

12.30 p.m. **Titchmarsh**
Alan takes things too far with guest Rebecca Loos and a set of ping-pong balls.

1.00 p.m. **Meerkats Under the Hammer**
Tragic mix-up in the BBC daytime commissioning department results in a grisly, yet watchable half hour.

1.30 p.m. **Midsomer Sexual Assaults**
Late-night version of the popular ITV show. Barnaby is called to the aftermath of a gay toga party in a beautifully restored Jacobean manor house.

3.00 p.m. **Celebrity Come Drink with Me**
Peter O'Toole mixes a bucket of cocktails for Gazza, Mel Gibson, Amy Winehouse and Lindsay Lohan.

4.00 p.m. **Not Going Out**
Since the BBC cancelled it.

5.00 p.m. **Diagnosis Nepotism**
Starring Dick van Dyke, Barry van Dyke, Jenny Harris-van Dyke and Oliver van Dyke. Directed by Mary van Dyke.

6.00 p.m. The Real George Michael
Investigative reporter Jacques Peretti travels the world and discovers George Michael is both a homosexual and a user of the drug cannabis.

6.30 p.m. Murder Connections
Doon Mackichan voices a look at all the various movers and shakers involved in Lord Lucan's nanny's death and the peer's subsequent escape.

7.00 p.m. The Lost Poems of Abu Yaere
BBC4 documentary with more people working on it than will ever watch it.

7.30 p.m. Ivy League Angst
Film that doesn't translate for a British audience at all but is worth seeing basically because you get to see Natalie Portman's baps about thirty-five minutes in.

8.00 p.m. Imagine
Alan Yentob spends a week with Keith Chegwin to uncover the man behind the genius.

9.00 p.m. Celebrity Fonejacker
Russell Brand and Jonathan Ross ring up celebrities for a laugh.

9.30 p.m. Jeremy Clarkson Saves the Environment
New fifteen-part series. Jeremy hovers over a rainforest in a private jet to examine the damage done to the Amazon, with special guests the Bangkok Ping-Pong Ball Orchestra.

10.00 p.m. Celebrity How to Look Good Naked
Gok meets Ann Widdecombe.

11.00 p.m. Prince Harry's Pakistan
This week the ginger royal narrowly avoids starting a war.

11.30 p.m. World Crossword Championships
Ray Stubbs and Hazel Irvine present the afternoon's second round, live and uninterrupted from Aylesbury Library.

12.00 a.m. This Morning
Hosted by Chris and Ingrid Tarrant for as long as possible, until one of them storms off set.

1.30 a.m. Shitcom
The writers of *Teenage Kicks* and *The World According to Bex* join up with the team behind *Life of Riley* to try and reach a new low in televised comedy. Starring Jennie Eclair, Nicholas Lyndhurst and Blakey from *On the Buses*.

2.00 a.m. River Factory Cookbook
A series of microwave recipes for battery-farmed chickens.

3.00 a.m. Tom's Shoes
Soap set in a small shoe shop in Hemel Hempstead.

4.00 a.m. The South Bank Show
In the last ever episode, Melvyn Bragg profiles the comedian Norman Collier.

80. CELEBRITY SCENTS YOU'LL NEVER SEE

ARMAGEDDON by AHMADINEJAD

VACANT by DAVID BECKHAM

GARY GLITTER'S TOUCH OF CHILDREN

WAYNE ROONEY'S VIEUX FEMME

PIERS MORGAN'S SMUG

PETER CROUCH'S STREAK OF PISS

AGYNESS DEYN'S POINTLESS

HOT AIR from BORIS JOHNSON

NIL by WINEHOUSE

VOMIT from GAZZA

WHIFF OF ALCOHOL by CHARLES KENNEDY

DESPERATION from GORDON BROWN

RUSSELL BRAND'S INDISCRETION

HINT OF TALENT by VICTORIA BECKHAM

SHAMELESS by STRINGFELLOW

KEIRA KNIGHTLEY'S IRRITATING

PRINCE HARRY'S
Surprisingly Ginger

81. WORDS ALMOST NEVER FOUND IN ROMANTIC SONGS

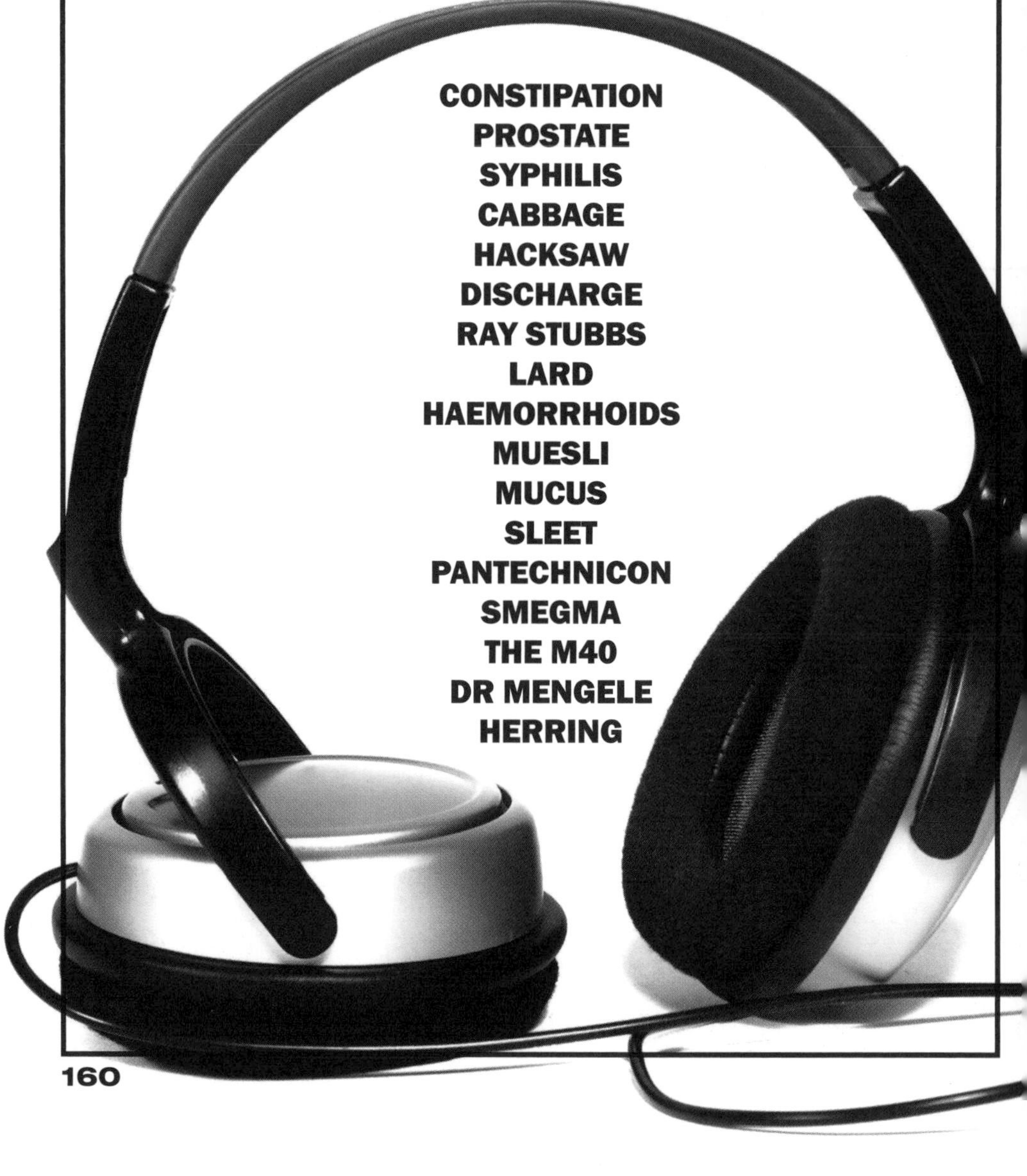

CONSTIPATION
PROSTATE
SYPHILIS
CABBAGE
HACKSAW
DISCHARGE
RAY STUBBS
LARD
HAEMORRHOIDS
MUESLI
MUCUS
SLEET
PANTECHNICON
SMEGMA
THE M40
DR MENGELE
HERRING